When I founded Mary Kay Cosmetics, I dreamed of offering an open-end opportunity to women everywhere. women just like you!

You've seized that opportunity with dedication and talent and made my dreams come true - for you!

As a true entrepreneur you are living your own success story! I'm so proud of you!

Love,
Mary Kay

THE ENTREPRENEURS

Books by Robert L. Shook

THE ENTREPRENEURS

TEN GREATEST SALESPERSONS

WINNING IMAGES

HOW TO BE THE COMPLETE
PROFESSIONAL SALESMAN
(WITH Herbert Shook)

TOTAL COMMITMENT
(WITH Ronald Bingamen)

THE
Entrepreneurs

Twelve Who Took Risks
and Succeeded

ROBERT L. SHOOK

HARPER & ROW, PUBLISHERS

NEW YORK

Cambridge   London
Hagerstown   Mexico
Philadelphia   São Paulo
San Francisco   1817   Sydney

Dedicated to Gerry and Jerry Schottenstein,
Happy 25th

I wish to express my appreciation to Richard Bartlett, Warren Cavior, Dwight Chapin, George Clifford, Nancy Cone, Kym Davick, Jeanne Desy, Frank Gorin, Bob Gorman, Mary Granius, Bill Haddad, Jan Hall, Robert Lazarus, Irv Levey, Mildred Lowmiller, Peggy Nordeen, Judy Otto, Jerry Schottenstein, Robert Shamansky, Herbert Shook, Mary Stanke, John Swisher, Gerry Ulmer, Karen Welsh, and Sonya Wolfe for their contributions to this book.

I am also very grateful to the wonderful entrepreneurs whom I have interviewed. They graciously volunteered their valuable time to share their philosophies, ideas, and stories with us.   R.L.S.

THE ENTREPRENEURS: TWELVE WHO TOOK RISKS AND SUCCEEDED. Copyright © 1980 by Robert L. Shook. All rights reserved. Printed in the United States of America. No part of this book may be used or reproduced in any manner whatsoever without written permission except in the case of brief quotations embodied in critical articles and reviews. For information address Harper & Row, Publishers, Inc., 10 East 53rd Street, New York, N.Y. 10022. Published simultaneously in Canada by Fitzhenry & Whiteside Limited, Toronto.

Designer: Sidney Feinberg

Library of Congress Cataloging in Publication Data

Shook, Robert L   1938–
    The entrepreneurs.
    1. Businessmen—United States—Biography.
    2. Women in business—United States—Biography.
    3. Entrepreneur. I. Title.
HC102.5.A2S5   1980   338′.04′0922   [B]
ISBN 0–06–014025–9   79–2735

80 81 82 83 84 10 9 8 7 6 5 4 3 2

Contents

Introduction

I believe that the most satisfying careers begin with an idea. Then the nourishing and developing of that idea can lead to the achievement of owning and operating a flourishing enterprise.

While an entrepreneur may acquire personal wealth in the process, that is not what's most significant. What's really important is the thrill of achievement, of seeing your idea unfold. The ultimate satisfaction lies in knowing that you worked hard and were smart and came out on top in the most competitive economic system in the world. And it's also satisfying to witness the contribution your successful business makes to others: your customers and your associates. I can't imagine a more fulfilling career.

The Entrepreneurs contains the stories of twelve men and women who have succeeded in building their own enterprises. Each started with an idea and hope. Some had an entirely new concept, while others took an old idea and made it better. Each believed that his or her product or service offered a better value to the consumer. And all were willing to make commitments to see their dreams become realities.

Obviously, with the estimated twelve million entrepreneurs

in the United States and Canada, I had a vast selection to choose from for this book. With such a large choice, I couldn't possibly include every deserving story, so it's important to note that *The Entrepreneurs* represents a cross-section of successful business owners in North America. My first criterion in choosing these twelve entrepreneurs was that they must be selfmade individuals. None of them had inherited wealth to invest in their businesses. Second, they all took great personal risks (an important part of the definition of *entrepreneur*). Finally, all are people of high integrity.

The American business community has come under attack in recent years, and I wanted to illustrate that honest business tactics can and do still work. Contrary to what many people believe, success in commerce and industry does not imply ruthlessness and deceitfulness. Furthermore, the American dream can still come true; opportunities are abundant. In fact, I selected several entrepreneurs who began their careers in the 1920s and 1930s to demonstrate that, regardless of economic conditions, there are always opportunities for the enterprising.

John W. Galbreath, one of the most successful real-estate entrepreneurs in the world, began his career in 1920 and prospered during the Great Depression of the thirties, a period when many people were content to take any kind of work just to have a job. W. Clement Stone, founder and chairman of the board of Combined Insurance Company of America, began his career in 1922 with a working capital of $100. He too refused to allow the Depression to defeat him, and his story tells how he turned it to his advantage. And Mary Hudson, the only woman in America to found an oil company, opened her first service station with $200 which she borrowed from her parents. Today Hudson Oil Company is the largest independent oil company in America.

Other businesses were founded more recently. Richard D. Schultz was twenty-two-years old when he organized National Revenue Corporation in 1973. Today his cash-flow management services firm is the largest of its kind in the world. S. Roger Horchow's business also started in 1973. Now the Horchow Collection is a household word. Gary Goranson founded Tidy Car, Inc., in 1976, and his franchised automobile-polishing service now has more than 2,000 associate dealers worldwide.

In 1963 Mary Kay Ash created Mary Kay Cosmetics, Inc. Today her company has more than 45,000 independent representatives, and it too is known in most American homes. In 1968 Dale W. Lang started Media Networks, Inc., which publishes local advertising pages for placement in national magazines. Every reader of major publications has seen many of these advertisements. JS&A Group, Inc., founded in 1971 by Joseph Sugarman, has become America's largest single source of space-age products.

In the agriculture industry, the success of William J. Richards, owner and president of Richards Farms, Inc., illustrates the farming opportunities in America. He began with a 325-acre farm in 1954 and, by his innovative farming techniques, has become one of America's most successful farmers.

In 1968 William G. McGowan founded MCI Communications Corporation, a telecommunications company competing with AT&T, which has traditionally had a monopoly on long-distance servicing. At first many people had serious doubts about his wisdom in meeting head-on with one of the world's largest companies. Another such entrepreneur, John Z. De Lorean, the founder of De Lorean Motor Company, was a top candidate for the presidency of General Motors. Now he is in the process of building what he hopes will be the first successful new American automobile company since Chrysler was founded in 1925. He too dares to challenge the giant corporations.

You will be reading about some of the most exciting business personalities in America. They are also among the luckiest people in the world—because every one of them thrives on his or her work. In addition to accumulating wealth as their businesses grow, they also derive immense enjoyment from their accomplishments. The "love of labor" is no myth—twelve times I witnessed it with these entrepreneurs.

These stories are unlike the hypothetical case histories found in textbooks. They are authentic stories about today's entrepreneurs—they are *real people*. Come share their experiences and discover their philosophies.

1

John W. Galbreath

(JOHN W. GALBREATH & CO.)

John W. Galbreath, one of America's most prominent real-estate developers, is chairman of the board of John W. Galbreath & Co., which he has operated in Columbus, Ohio, since 1924. He is the chairman of the board and principal owner of the Pittsburgh Pirates Baseball Club, and the owner of Darby Dan Farm, located in Galloway, Ohio, which consists of approximately 4,300 acres.

In Lexington, Kentucky, at a second Darby Dan Farm, he raises thoroughbred horses. His winning horses include Chateaugay (1963 Kentucky Derby and Belmont Stakes), Proud Clarion (1967 Kentucky Derby), Little Current (1974 Preakness and Belmont Stakes), and Roberto (1972 Epsom Derby, in England). He is the first American to win both the Kentucky Derby and the Epsom Derby.

John entered the real-estate business in Columbus, Ohio, in 1920. His present principal offices are in Columbus, Pittsburgh, and New York.

He purchases, rehabilitates, sells, and manages many industrial townsites, including fifteen townsites in the vicinity of Uniontown, Pennsylvania; eight townsites near Birmingham, Alabama; eight townsites in Utah, New Mexico, and Nevada; the townsites of Mineville, Port Henry, and Lyon Mountain, New York; the townsite of Dragerton, Utah; the townsite of Henderson, Nevada; the townsite of

Fairless Hills, Pennsylvania (consisting of over 2,000 residences, a shopping center, and other facilities, built to serve the Fairless Works of United States Steel Corporation); the townsites of Hoyt Lakes, Silver Bay, and Babbitt, Minnesota (serving the taconite industry); an addition of 200 houses to the village of Woodsfield, Ohio (to serve the Olin Corporation); housing developments consisting of several hundred houses located in Lorain and McDonald, Ohio; and the complete new town of Kearny, Arizona (consisting of approximately 700 units serving the Kennecott Copper Corporation).

John has also built an office building in Weirton, West Virginia, for Weirton Steel Company; a home office in New York City for the Continental Can Company; a 5,000-acre "Satellite City" (Bramalea) outside Toronto, Canada, to serve the expanding Toronto population and new industries in the area; Erieview Urban Redevelopment in Cleveland; a forty-two-story office building in Pittsburgh, now principally occupied by Mellon National Bank; the Socony-Mobil Building in New York City, principally occupied by Mobil Oil Company; an office building in Fairfield, Alabama, occupied by Tennessee Coal and Iron Division of United States Steel Corporation; an office building in Chicago, principally occupied by Sinclair Oil Company; an office building in Boston, under lease to International Business Machines Corporation; an office and research laboratory near Boston, for Radio Corporation of America.

His company owns eight separate sales and distribution facilities located throughout the country under lease to Standard Brands, Inc., as well as bakeries in Los Angeles and Sacramento for Continental Baking Company. He owns and/or has developed the following properties: an office and warehouse in Providence, under lease to St. Regis Paper Company; offices and warehouses in Detroit, Los Angeles, and Grand Rapids under lease to Owens-Corning Fiberglas Corporation; a sixty-four-story office building in Pittsburgh for United States Steel Corporation; an office building (thirty-two stories) in Cincinnati; a twenty-seven-story office building in Toledo; an office building (twenty-four stories) in Akron; Erieview Tower (forty stories) in Cleveland—principal tenant, Ohio Bell Telephone Company; an office building (twenty-four stories) in Columbus—principal tenant,

Bank One Corporation; One Liberty Plaza (fifty-four stories) in New York City (one of twelve winners of the Architectural Awards of Excellence)—principal tenant, Merrill Lynch, Pierce, Fenner & Smith, Inc.; Union Bank Square (forty stories) in Los Angeles, a joint venture with Connecticut General Life Insurance Company; an office building (thirty-four stories) in Columbus—principal tenant, Borden, Inc.; an office building in Columbus for the Nationwide Insurance Company; an office building in Louisville for the First National City Bank; offices (two towers, forty-three and twenty-eight stories) in San Francisco; Market-Mohawk urban-renewal project in Columbus, consisting of various office buildings, stores, a motel, high-rise apartments, and restaurants; Westminster Terrace, an urban-renewal project in Columbus; Mei Foo Sun Chuen, the largest housing project ever built by private industry, which will ultimately house 80,000 people in Kowloon, Hong Kong.

Some of the many honors he has received are the Horatio Alger Award (1960); the Founders' Citation of Ohio University (1967); Marketing Man of the Year (1969) from the Central Ohio Chapter of the American Marketing Association; 1972 Columbus Realtor of the Year from the Columbus Board of Realtors; 1972 Ohio Realtor of the Year from the Ohio Association of Real Estate Boards; Man of the Year for 1972, awarded by the Thoroughbred Racing Association; the Joe Palmer Award for meritorious service to racing by the National Turf Writers' Association; Christopher Columbus Award (1973); the Ernie Godfrey Award of Distinction (1974) from the Columbus Chapter of the National Football Foundation and Hall of Fame; the Eclipse Award (1975) presented by the Thoroughbred Racing Association and the National Turf Writers' Association for owning the 1974 champion three-year-old colt and for being that year's outstanding breeder; the Dean Eagle Award (1975) for outstanding contribution to the thoroughbred racing industry; the P. A. B. Widener Trophy (1975); Outstanding Breeder for 1974 from the New York Turf Writers' Association. On August 19, 1975, Galbreath was honored as one of the most distinguished citizens of Columbus, Ohio; officials named a small park in Columbus the John W. Galbreath Square.

He has received the following honorary degrees: Honorary LL.D. from Athens College, Athens, Alabama, 1956; Honorary LL.D. from Ohio University, Athens, Ohio, 1957; Doctor of Business Administration from Ohio Northern University, 1960; Honorary LL.D. from Ohio State University, 1971; Doctor of Humanities, Springfield College, Springfield, Massachusetts, 1975; Honorary Doctor of Humanities from Ohio Dominican College in Columbus, Ohio, 1977.

He has served on the board of directors of City National Bank & Trust Co., Buckeye Federal Savings & Loan Association, Bank One Corporation, and Buckeye International, all of Columbus, Ohio; Churchill Downs, Inc., of Louisville, Kentucky.

He is the past president of the Columbus Real Estate Board, Ohio Real Estate Association, and the National Association of Realtors.

He served on the board of trustees of Ohio University from 1941 to 1976. In addition, he is involved with the following organizations: Cancer Fund, Center of Science and Industry, Children's Hospital, Columbus Foundation, Columbus Gallery of Fine Arts, Columbus Academy, Columbus Symphony Orchestra, Inc., First Community Church (gave land for a church camp in memory of his first wife, Helen Mauck Galbreath), Ohio State University Equine Research, Ohio State University Development Fund, and Ohio State University Fund.

John was born in Derby, Ohio, on August 10, 1897. After serving in the U.S. Army as a second lieutenant during World War I, he graduated from Ohio University in 1920. He has two children, Joan Phillips and Daniel M. Galbreath. He and his wife, Dorothy, live on Darby Dan Farm, in Galloway, Ohio.

"This is an intriguing business," declares John W. Galbreath. "I guess it's the only business in the world where no two products are exactly alike. I can sell you a house today, and the house next to it could be completely different. Or it might be a vacant lot that's different from the lot next to it. One may be on a corner; one may have greater depth. No two things in the real-estate business are alike, and every one of them is a different challenge."

The preceding comments could have been made by some eager, bushy-tailed young salesman who just received his first commission check from a residential closing. But that's the brand of enthusiasm that John Galbreath, one of the world's most prominent real-estate developers, injects into the business every day, and he's been at it for almost sixty years! There's no question that he still possesses the same love of labor that he did when he began selling real estate in 1920 immediately after his graduation from Ohio University.

"I had $100 to my name, and I used it to purchase a Ford," he says with a warm smile. "A college pal of mine had graduated a year ahead of me, and I joined the real-estate firm he worked for in Columbus. I started in the business like any other salesperson. I knew nothing about real estate, but I certainly had a strong desire to learn. I worked at least twelve to fourteen hours every day, and Saturdays and Sundays were no exception. And I was a real student of the business— I absorbed all the books about real estate that I could get my hands on. It was a nightly ritual for me to stay up and study until the wee hours of the morning."

John pauses briefly and then emphasizes: "It's really that simple. I don't care what field we're talking about. It takes that kind of determination if an individual wants to get ahead in this world. I *lived* real estate, breathed it day and night. And I'll tell you something else: I used to drive 50,000 miles a year looking at real estate, finding listings of properties. I'd have to buy a new car every year. I went up and down every street in Columbus looking at houses, and I knew every country road in the county because I was also interested in farmland."

John soon began to sell commercial properties in addition to his residential listings. Four years after entering the real-estate business, he formed his own company, John W. Galbreath & Co.

"I guess I just migrated into the commercial end of the business," he explains. "We sold a lot of houses, and, of course, we wanted to grow and expand. Gradually we got into doubles and apartment units. We just kept moving into that area; whatever anybody listed with us, we'd consider. We kept meeting more people, and it was simply a matter of expansion to the more sophisticated listings. That's all."

John tells how his business flourished during the 1920s, and how he gradually established good working relationships with the financial institutions of the business community. "If you have a feasible deal, there's never any problem about financing," he insists, "because that's what all the savings-and-loan companies, life-insurance companies, and banks are in business for! So, if a real-estate person has anything practical that makes sense, he's not going to have any trouble finding a

JOHN W. GALBREATH

loan commitment. And the same thing is true today when we develop large office buildings."

In 1929 the Great Depression hit, bringing in its wake millions of foreclosures. Many formerly successful businesses failed. John was determined that he would not become another casualty. "I used to ride through the country in my car figuring out how to lick this thing," he reminisces. "I had all kinds of job offers. Life-insurance companies that had taken title on thousands of properties were after me to manage them, and so were other big companies that owned a lot of real estate. I can't begin to tell you how real-estate sales activities dropped during the Depression! A lot of people who had been successful in their own businesses were taking any job that was available. And, of course, if that was their philosophy or what they had to do, I don't see anything wrong with it. But I felt differently and I was determined to stay with it. Well, I developed a plan whereby the people with money could buy distressed properties; then I started finding them properties in Columbus, Cleveland, Akron, Wooster. Soon I was working everywhere. You see, I was dealing with people of substance who had the money and staying power to see this thing through. When the economy improved, my plan worked out beautifully, and that's the way I got started in the business.

"I can remember sitting down with the chairman of the board of one of the biggest life-insurance companies in the country at the tail end of the Depression," John continues. "He told me that though it was unfortunate that people must lose their property, his company had to take title and repossess. He was very sympathetic, but he didn't feel that financial institutions were actually taking advantage of anybody. It was simply a case of people who couldn't carry on, and they were happy to get rid of the burden. The chairman said that his company made money in every recession and depression. I have found that to be true of all of the savings-and-loan companies, the banks, and the insurance companies that took properties back on foreclosures, because they then sold these properties for more than the existing mortgages. Their mortgages were safe even when they had to have a public sale at the courthouse.

"Some of these institutions all of a sudden wound up with 700 or 800 properties to manage, and this, I believe, was the turning point as far as my firm was concerned," John continues. "I believed that the future of our country was solid and sound. I felt that part of the real problem in Germany during the 1920s was that the people were exploited by landlords. The Germans had serious shortages; they had to pay exorbitant rents, far beyond what they could reasonably afford. After the Depression our country, being the greatest home-ownership country in the world, depended on real-estate values coming back. I persuaded the financial institutions and individuals that owned large downtown properties to allow me to sell them great blocks of real estate containing as many as 100 to 200 houses, without their having to put up any additional money—just additional security. I then told them to take those houses on a long-term payout and maintain them until the Depression was over. Well, they did, and later on there was great demand for the houses. We made many deals like that, and not a single buyer ever lost a dime. They all made money because they had the staying power to carry over. As the Depression came to a close, we received large cash commissions on the deals we closed.

"We then started buying company towns from the big corporations that wanted to get rid of the properties they had had for so many years. You see, these company towns were at one time a necessity because when the railroads were first built across America and other industries sprang up, the only way the companies could get people to work for them was to supply them with housing. This situation was true of all big industry. The steel companies, for example, owned town after town—everything, lock, stock, and barrel, including the stores. I remember once talking with John L. Lewis, who told me that he believed in private ownership as much as anyone, but he recognized that at one time company towns were a necessity. Well, I understood housing, and I believed in home ownership *more than anything else in the world.* And I knew that after the Depression somebody had to help the financial institutions get rid of all their properties.

"I went to these big coal and steel companies, and I told them that when you give a person a deed to his house, you make a really great citizen out of him. *You make him an American!* There's nothing more important in a democracy than home ownership. When a citizen owns his own home, he has a piece of his country. It was simply amazing how home ownership affected people. The rate of absenteeism dropped off 22 percent, and you can imagine what that meant to these industrial corporations. The change of attitudes showed in the factories. Another exciting thing that happened was the pride of ownership that the people developed. We took movies of 'before' and 'after' in one town, and we observed how these proud homeowners worked on their homes and lawns. They added on rooms, built garages, and the real-estate values of the community increased dramatically."

John grins. "An old lady in one of these towns approached me and said, 'I'm in the twilight of my life. Are you saying to me, Mr. Galbreath, that if I own this home nobody can ever take it away from me?' I told her that was correct—except in the rare exception if the government condemned it—nobody could take it away from her. With that, she counted out $4,200 in old $20 gold certificates and bought the house."

Some people may choose to believe John W. Galbreath & Co. got its big break in the Depression. Perhaps it was more a case of making a disadvantage become an advantage. While the majority of people were taking a defeatist attitude during the 1930s, John sought opportunities instead of accepting failure. And consequently he provided a definite service, because not only were the financial institutions in dire need of his expertise but he also made it possible for thousands and thousands of Americans to become homeowners. After the Depression, John W. Galbreath emerged as a highly successful real-estate entrepreneur, and his outstanding performance won him a reputation that he cherishes.

"You've got to earn your spurs!" John asserts. "I don't care what business one is in, one has to be able to live up to one's standards. When I started selling houses, it was important for me to develop a meaningful relationship with the local financial institutions. I'd have a client make an application at a building-and-loan company, and we'd do the same thing when we got into building homes. I got to know people, and after we'd been doing business for a while it was up to them to evaluate me and make a decision as to whether or not they wanted to continue to do business with me. Over a period of time an individual will establish a reputation for himself, and if it's a good one, he's going to prosper.

"For example," he continues, "I can remember one time when I told an institution that there was an extra bathroom in a house. Later they were taking an inventory and they discovered that there was only one bathroom. When they told me about it, I didn't say a word to them, but instead I went out and built another room on and put a bath in it, without ever telling them until it was completed. Then I went to them and said, 'You look at it now. It now has two baths.' Well, that mistake cost me almost $3,000, but I had to do it; a man's word has got to be the law.

"I don't care what kind of deal it is," he adds. "A good while ago I had a $7.5 million deal, and the gentleman said to me as I got up to leave his office, 'Say, John, don't you want me to sign something?' I told him, 'No. You told me to do it and I'll do it.' Well, I did, and we closed the deal without ever having a contract."

John emphasizes seriously, "That does not come easy. It comes out of fifty years of hard work and trying to make your word good. But that's true in any business, not just mine. That's what business is based on!"

John believes that an individual's reputation will give him the necessary credibility, and sometimes it may even mean *turning down business in order to generate future business.* "I think that one of the smartest things in business is being able to say no," John insists. "Several years ago we were offered an exclusive listing for a $12 million property located in a downtown city, and we wouldn't take it. I also said that we wouldn't want the embarrassment of having to come back a year later without having sold it for them. About a year and a half passed, and I went to see them and said, 'I think there's a good chance to sell the property now. Would you like us to work on it?' They told me that they were interested, and within six months we sold it—all cash.

"You see," he points out, "when times got better, I thought that I could sell it, and I did. Just imagine the respect they now have for a real-estate broker who wouldn't want to list a $12 million property. They couldn't believe it! We get deals brought to us from all over the world, and I would estimate that we'll only take about one third of them. Our mail is full of people wanting us to list their properties all of the time. Just last week we got a beautiful piece of property out in California."

One of John's favorite principles is: *The key to success in business is to know your business better than the other fellow knows it.* "It comes from being totally committed to your work," he stresses. "And when you *do* know your business better than anyone else, the other person is going to know that you do. I remember an occasion when I had to make a presentation to a board of directors of a big Wall Street company. They wanted me to come down and tell them how to do a certain project. Well, I got halfway through my speech, and the chairman interrupted me and said, 'Look, we know you know what you're talking about. You got the job!' And that was a $30 million construction job. Now, I don't know how that happened. I can't really tell you exactly what it was that I said, but I do know that *they knew* that *I knew* what I was talking about, so it wasn't necessary for me to go on any further.

"It all gets back to three things," John simplifies. "First, people have to like you, so you must start with that. Second, you have to know more about your subject than anyone else. Third, you must dedicate your time completely to doing the job that you're committed to do. Once you do a good job, everybody else will know about it. But if you do one bad job, no matter if you did twenty good ones, they never forget the bad one!"

John admits that as soon as he became active in the real-estate field, he had intentions of doing things on a big scale. He's never been known to shy away from a project because it was too big. "I believe it's actually easier to do business with people who think big than to work on little deals. You don't have to penny-pinch with them, and they're not always arguing about little things, the way small homeowners tend to do." He's also willing to put his own money into any project that he develops. "We work on a fee basis for our clients, and we're also willing to put some equity money into what we develop," he explains. "A lot of corporations think that if we have our own money in it, we'll be looking out for theirs at the same time we're looking out for our own. Well, that's not true because whether we have anything in it or not isn't really an issue. We always have the same interest in doing the best possible job. We have a good reputation which we cherish, and we do each project as if our reputation were on the line."

Now John W. Galbreath & Co. is engaged in the final phase of a joint venture with the Mobil Oil Corporation and the Turner Construction Company. The project is the Mei Foo Sun Chuen housing complex in Kowloon, Hong Kong, which will ultimately house 80,000 people. It is a planned community consisting of ninety-nine twenty-story buildings with 400 elevators on a thirty-seven-acre site, including shopping malls, schools, and recreational facilities.

"The Mobil Oil Company (whose home office is in one of the office buildings we built in New York) owned this property in Hong Kong," John says with obvious pride. "After having known us for many years, they came to us explaining that they didn't know quite what to do with this piece of land. Well, I spent seven weeks in Hong Kong studying it. So I knew when I met with Mobil's chairman of the board that the property was right for this Mei Foo Sun Chuen housing complex. I was convinced that the middle-class people in Hong Kong had never had the opportunity to own anything, and I persuaded Mobil that to offer them the chance to have their own homes could be a very profitable venture.

"I also had met with the governor of the island, and he informed me, 'Mr. Galbreath, we have to house 1,800,000 people here in the next ten years.' That was all he had to tell me, and I then met with all the banks and everybody else," John continues. "At first, a lot of people, including the governor, were somewhat skeptical, because the site was a thirty-seven-acre parcel that sat on top of a tank farm full of oil tanks.

"You should see it now," he says, beaming. "It's absolutely beautiful. The view is magnificent; we have a big frontage on the bay. The place is clean, because with so many people in such concentration, well, we'd have a problem otherwise. We even made machines to pick up chewing gum! Yeah, it even dissolves the gum too."

John laughs. "I take enormous pride in this Mei Foo Sun Chuen project because it's the biggest single housing development that's ever been built by private industry. There are absolutely no public funds in it. When we first began developing it, a lot of people didn't believe it would succeed. One of the big banks over there wouldn't go along with it in the early stages, but when we were about halfway through, they approached us and said that they had made a mistake. 'We want to come in now,' they said. We told them that we had two banks in the deal already and our agreement with them was that no other bank would be allowed to participate. The bank told us that if they could get the other two banks to give us a written release, and if we would agree to it, then they would buy $50 million worth of our mortgage paper without recourse! Now, I really was pleased with that, and I derive a great sense of accomplishment from the entire project."

Perhaps the thoroughness of his preparation prior to making a business commitment is the single trait that most impresses anyone who observes John in action. "There's an old story I once heard," he says with a smile, "about a boy who flunked out of college and was scared to go home to tell his father. Instead, he sent his father's best friend a wire which read, 'Flunked out. Be home tomorrow. Prepare Dad.' He got back a wire that said, 'Dad's prepared. Prepare yourself.' And that's the whole story. You've got to be prepared. That's the basis for all of it. You just have to know more about your business, and there's nothing more disrespectful or presumptuous than going into another person's office and not being able to make it worth his time. If you are not able to answer all of his questions, then you've wasted his time—and your own. You owe him an apology.

"I recall a time during the 1940s when a large corporation went into a community in the South, where they wanted to build a plant. The Chamber of Commerce turned the prospect over to a broker, and the company representatives started asking him a million questions about this and that. About a third of their questions were answered by the broker: 'I don't know.' The company got so provoked that they approached another town of approximately the same size, about fifty miles away. The broker in that town knew everything! He said, 'Now, if you build your plant, it should be located here because you'll get a different tax base than you have in this spot.' I mean, that guy answered everything! The company ended up building in the second town, and it employed about 4,500 people; it's still going. Now, there's the difference being prepared is going to make. Either you go into it prepared or you'd better stay away!"

One of John's favorite stories stressing preparedness is about his son, Dan. "I kept hammering the importance of being prepared to Dan when he first came into our business," John relates with great pleasure, "and, fortunately, he got the message right away. Dan and I were negotiating a deal with the president of a large corporation about our developing a $6 million building for them on a lease-back arrangement. With a deal of this nature, you must be exact with the interest rates and the amount of rent you're talking about. One decimal-point fluctuation in the interest rate can have a tremendous dollar effect on rent over ten or twenty years. So prior to meeting with the company I suggested to Dan that he memorize the rent tables covering the spread between 3.5 and 5.5 percent interest.

"And, don't you know it, as we got into the last stages of negotiating, the corporation president asked us to calculate several different rent figures based on different interest rates. He must have expected us to ask to borrow his calculator, but instead Dan started rattling off the figures on the different rents figured at the various interest rates. Naturally, the president realized that Dan had done his homework before sitting down at the meeting. Certainly he knew that nobody could calculate interest rates that fast in his head. But he was obviously impressed that Dan had come to the meeting so well prepared. Dan had won his respect and he had confidence in us—enough so that we got the job."

John Galbreath has spent most of a lifetime in the real-estate development field. Light on his feet, he's been able to weather the storms and keep his firm prosperous during economic slumps. And, most important, he keeps up with the times. In fact, it could be said that he's been a pace-setter in his industry. John believes that real estate still offers many fine opportunities. "It's tragic, however," he comments, "that the government has almost doubled the capital-gains tax. Our government is so uninformed that they don't know that, although they doubled it, they're only getting about half as much money as they did when we were paying half of what it is now! There's just no desire to sell property if you can't keep any of the profits that you made over the years in developing the property; so people are just holding on to it. And the high capital-gains tax removes the incentive from taking the risk because you're going to end up giving 70 percent of your profits to the government."

Of course, John has witnessed many changes in every facet of the real-estate business during the past sixty years, and he's convinced that government policy and business conditions are always subject to change. In the long run, he has great confidence in the future of America.

As far as John Galbreath's future is concerned, he's planning to continue at about the same pace as usual. "My son and I are here by 8:30 every morning," he claims, "and we're generally the last two people to leave at the end of the day. I feel just like a horse in the Fire Department. When the bell rings, when a new deal comes up that has a challenge in it, I still get all excited about it.

"Yeah," he concludes, with enthusiasm, "I could tell you stories you wouldn't believe about the fun of doing something—and then seeing it come out right."

2

W. Clement Stone

(COMBINED INSURANCE COMPANY OF AMERICA)

W. Clement Stone is chairman of the board of Combined Insurance Company of America. In 1922, with a working capital of $100, he established his own one-man insurance agency under the name Combined Registry Company. In 1939 he acquired the management contract of the American Casualty Company (now Combined American Insurance Company) of Dallas, of which he became president. The same year he organized the Combined Mutual Casualty Company in Chicago. He became president and general manager of the Combined Casualty Company of Des Moines in 1940. By 1946 he had acquired the Pennsylvania Casualty Company of Philadelphia, a stock company licensed to sell accident and health insurance.

After changing the name of his Philadelphia insurance firm to Combined Insurance Company of America, he merged Combined Mutual Casualty Company into this firm. In addition to being chairman of the board of Combined American Insurance Company, he is chairman of the board and chief executive officer of Combined Insurance Company of Wisconsin. He is also chairman of the board of Combined Opportunities, Inc. (a Minority Enterprise Small Business Investment Corporation); chairman of the board and president of Combined Life Insurance Company of New York; chairman of the board of Success Unlimited, Inc., a Chicago publishing company;

and a director of the Alberto-Culver Company.

The business and professional associations in which he has taken part over the years include: American Life Insurance Association; American Management Association, New York; Chicago Association of Commerce and Industry; Chicago Association of Health Underwriters; Executives Club of Chicago; Illinois State Chamber of Commerce; Insurance Federation of Illinois; Insurance Hall of Fame; International Association of Health Underwriters, Chicago; International Insurance Seminars; Sales Marketing Executives of Chicago, Inc.; Sales Marketing Executives International, Inc., New York; Society of Midland Authors; United States Chamber of Commerce; national policy advisory committee of United Shareholders of America, New York; advisory board of Broader Urban Involvement and Leadership Development, Inc. (BUILD); board of directors of the Horatio Alger Awards Committee; Chicago Committee of the Chicago Council on Foreign Relations; Citizens of Greater Chicago; and The Hundred Club of Cook County. He is a sponsoring associate of the Foreign Policy Association; vice-chairman of the National Center for Voluntary Action; a member of the board of directors of the National Conference of Christians and Jews Regional Board, Chicago Area; and a member of the advisory council of the Uptown Chicago Commission.

He is a member of the American Australian Association; life member of the Kiwanis Club of the North Shore, Chicago, and Kiwanis International; 33-degree Mason of the Ancient Accepted Scottish Rite, Valley of Chicago; University of Illinois Presidents' Club, Urbana; board of governors of the Variety Club of Illinois; and a patron life member of Variety International.

He belongs to the Art Institute of Chicago; the Chicago Planetarium Society; the Evanston Historical Society; the Sarah Siddons Society, Chicago. He is an honorary director of the Chicago Chamber Orchestra Association; director and member of the Lyric Guild, Lyric Opera of Chicago; and an honorary member of the Newberry Library Associates.

He is a member of the advisory council of the Everett M. Dirksen Republican Forum; a trustee of the Lincoln Academy of Illinois; a member of the National Advisory Council on Minority Business Enterprise; on the executive committee of the Republican National Finance Committee; a trustee of the Robert A. Taft Institute of Government; a trustee of United Republican Fund of Illinois, Chicago; a member of the American Association for Maternal and Child Health, Inc., Chicago; a member of the board of governors of the Chicago Heart Association; chairman of the board of Helping Hearts and Hands, Chicago; a trustee of the Illinois Masonic Medical Center; a citizen fellow of the Institute of Medicine; a board director of the International College of Surgeons; an honorary trustee of the Massachusetts Eye and Ear Infirmary, Boston; a sponsor of Mayo Foundation Development Program; and a director of the American Hearing Research Foundation.

He is also a member of the Menninger Foundation, Topeka, Kansas; the National Association for Mental Health; and the World Federation for Mental Health. He is chairman of the board of the Institutes of Religion and Health, New York; chairman of the advisory board of the Pastoral Counseling Center, New York; a director of The Villages; a member of the advisory committee of the Katherine Wright Mental Health Clinic, Chicago; a member of the advisory board for the Lewis University Special Services Center, Chicago; a director of the Guides for Better Living Correctional Program; a director of the John Howard Association, Chicago; a member of the Burden Neurological Institute, Bristol, England; a director of the Foundation for Research on the Nature of Man, Durham, North Carolina; honorary chairman, Foundation for the Study of Cycles, Pittsburgh; a trustee of the Urological Research Foundation, College of Medicine, University of Utah; a member and trustee of the First United Presbyterian Church of Evanston, Illinois; on the board of directors of the Laymen's National Bible Committee, New York; a director of the Protestant Foundation of Greater Chicago; and president and trustee of the Religious Heritage of America, Inc., Washington, D.C.

Stone's present and past participation in many youth and education groups include: patron of Boystown, Auckland, New Zealand; a member of the National Executive Committee of the Boys' Clubs of America, New York; sustaining member of the Boy Scouts of America, Evanston Council, Illinois; chairman of the board of Chicago Boys' Clubs; trustee of Chicago Educational Television Association, WTTW; chairman of the board of trustees of Interlochen Arts Academy and the National Music Camp, Michigan; chairman of the board of trustees of the International Council on Education for Teaching (ICET); life member and member of the board of managers of the Robert R. McCormick Chicago Boys Club; advisory committee member of the National Football Foundation and Hall of Fame, Inc., New York; honorary trustee of Southwest Baptist College, Bolivar, Missouri; advisory board of Teen Challenge, New York; trustee of George Williams College, Downers Grove, Illinois; and trustee of Pop Warner Little Scholars, Philadelphia. He is affiliated with the Keystone (International) Boys' Clubs.

He holds many honorary degrees: Doctor of Humane Letters, DePaul University (1970); Doctor of Humanities, Interlochen Arts Academy, Michigan (1964); Doctor of Humanities, Whitworth College, Brookhaven, Mississippi (1969); Doctor of Humanities, Southwest Baptist College, Bolivar, Missouri (1970); Doctor of Humanities, Lincoln College, Lincoln, Illinois (1971); Doctor of Jurisprudence, Monmouth College, Monmouth, Illinois (1963); Doctor of Laws, Whittier College, Whittier, California (1973); Doctor of Letters, National College of Chiropractic, Lombard, Illinois (1969); and Doctor of Public Service, Salem College, Salem, West Virginia (1974).

Stone has received many special awards including: Layman of the Year from Religious Heritage of America (1962); Horatio Alger Award (1963); Church Layman of the Year, presented by the Church Federation of Greater Chicago (1968); the Daniel A. Lord Award from the Loyola Academy (1968); the Boys' Club Golden Keystone Award from the Boys' Clubs of America (1968); the Robert S. Solinsky Award from the Illinois Institute of Applied Behavioral Science (1968); the B'nai B'rith National Humanitarian Award (1968); Special Citation, National Bible Week, from the Laymen's National Bible Committee (1968); Patron of the Year Award from the Chicago Medical School's Department of Microbiology (1969); the St. Vincent DePaul Award from DePaul University (1970); Humanities Award from the College of Insurance (1971). He received the Free

Enterprise Exemplar Medal from the Freedoms Foundation (1972); the Royal Arch Gold Medal Award of the General Grand Chapter, Royal Arch Masons International (1972); the State of Israel Prime Minister's Award (1972); and the Foster G. and Mary W. McGaw Award (1974).

Stone is the author or co-author of several books published by Prentice-Hall: *The Success System That Never Fails* (1962); *Success Through a Positive Mental Attitude* (1960) with Napoleon Hill; and *The Other Side of the Mind* (1964) with Norma Lee Browning.

He is chairman of the W. Clement and Jessie V. Stone Foundation. At the end of 1978 his personal gifts and family foundation grants exceeded $100 million.

He was born on May 4, 1902, in Chicago, Illinois. He married his high-school sweetheart, Jessie Verna Tarson. They have three children, Clement, Norman, and Donna, and live in a suburb of Chicago.

W. CLEMENT STONE

On a damp, chilly day in 1908 a scared six-year-old boy was selling newspapers on Chicago's tough South Side. Upon being chased away from a busy corner by older newspaper boys, the lad nervously entered Hoelle's Restaurant, a busy and prosperous establishment.

After having made a lucky sale at the first table, and then at the second and third tables, the frightened youngster was ushered out by Mr. Hoelle. However, the youth had sold three newspapers, so when Mr. Hoelle wasn't looking, he quickly rushed in to sell to a fourth customer. The jovial customer liked the boy's gumption and, in addition to purchasing a newspaper, gave him a ten-cent tip. Again Mr. Hoelle pushed him out. With four newspapers sold and a ten-cent bonus, the boy again entered the restaurant. The customers, who had been enjoying the show, burst into laughter. "Let him be," they shouted as Mr. Hoelle approached the young entrepreneur; within five minutes all the papers were sold.

The next evening the boy again entered the restaurant; again Mr. Hoelle showed him the front door. But the second time he walked in, Mr. Hoelle threw his arms in the air and exclaimed, "What's the use!" The two of them became good friends, and each evening thereafter the young boy sold his newspapers at Hoelle's Restaurant.

Practicing these same principles and work habits, W. Clement Stone proceeded to build one of America's greatest insurance-company empires.

"As a young boy, I had a need for money," Stone recalls. "And the newspapers that I had purchased to resell had no value whatsoever if they weren't sold. I couldn't even read them! I was motivated to avoid what seemed, at the time, like a total disaster. So I had the necessary *inspiration to action.* When I dared to re-enter the restaurant after selling three papers, I began to develop a necessary technique; I began to possess *know-how.* I had heard the older boys yell out headlines, so I simply repeated in a softer voice what I had heard. I call this *activity knowledge.*

"Since that time," Stone says with a smile, "I have employed the same techniques to develop what I refer to as my 'system for success.' The elements of *inspiration to action, know-how,* and *activity knowledge* are proven factors to acquiring fortunes."

Stone and his widowed mother moved from Chicago to Detroit where she opened an insurance agency representing the United States Casualty Company. She pawned her two diamonds to add to the capital she needed to start her business. The agency became known as the Liberty Registry Company. The boy visited his mother in Detroit during his summer vacations. While in his teens, he started his selling career there by selling low-premium accident policies for the agency. This was the beginning of a career that would eventually take him to the top of one of America's largest industries.

"At the age of twenty," Stone recalls, "I started my own agency, Combined Registry Company, which specialized in a low-cost product that I believed everyone needed. My philosophy has always been to sell a necessity with a price that everyone can afford, and to sell it in volume. Of course, what is more of a necessity than insurance? This is particularly true of accident insurance, because every man, woman, and child can use such protection. So, theoretically, you can start small and then expand. My philosophy has always been to sell a necessity that repeats—and certainly an insurance policy does that because of its renewal feature.

"In those days the cost was relatively low, because the travel-accident policy would cover being injured in public conveyances, autos, and being run over on the highway, and so on. It was sold to a man and his wife and even the children. It was easy to sell in volume because we would go where the money is—mostly places like offices, banks, and large department stores. I felt that the majority of insurance agents selling similar coverage went to places where there wasn't any money—they called on poor people! I can remember when I averaged seventy-two policies per day for nine working days. During that period my best day was 122 sales.

"In my second year of business I suddenly resolved that I was going to *multiply* myself," Stone continues. "The night after I had sold 122 policies, I found myself selling in my sleep. That's when I decided that because my restlessness was not conducive to a healthy mind, I was going to build an organization. At the time I was living in Chicago, so I put a four-line ad in the *Tribune*. The response was terrific! I was amazed to have so many applicants call my office, but even more astonished at the large numbers of people who responded outside of Chicago, from Wisconsin, Indiana, Michigan, downstate Illinois, and elsewhere. I suddenly realized the fine opportunities that existed to expand beyond Chicago and even beyond Illinois."

Stone was able to obtain permission from the New Amsterdam Casualty Company to recruit agents from other states. Soon he began building a national sales force. The company was so pleased with his production that he later obtained exclusive rights to a special accident policy to be sold nationally. He dubbed it "The Little Giant" to symbolize a lot of protection for little cost. The name still stands on some of his present policies with similar coverage.

Using the same success formula that worked in generating his own personal production, Stone began building the agency with the philosophy, "What the mind of man can conceive and believe, the mind of man can achieve."

"I don't care what field an individual works in," he stresses, "anyone who is truly successful develops a formula and scientifically follows a game plan. I developed a successful sales presentation, and I told every man and woman who came to work for me, 'If you do exactly as I tell you, you can't fail! Look, you don't have to believe a thing. I will *prove* it to you. And when I get you licensed, I'll prove that you can do it too.' I would personally demonstrate in any business section they chose how easy it was to sell in volume. I kept on emphasizing, 'It's impossible to fail—absolutely impossible!' I would even offer large sums of money to anyone who could show me one failure of any individual in our organization who followed the system.

"And if there was a salesperson or a manager who wasn't producing in an area, I would go out in the field to prove that there was a bonanza in his territory. For example, we had one man in Laredo, Texas, who claimed that our insurance couldn't be sold to Mexicans. I went down there to inspect personally. You see, I believe that you don't always get what you *expect* unless you *inspect*. I worked with the manager in a complete city block, and he would look at a place of business and say, 'I can't sell in there.' Well, he was right—*he* couldn't! On the last call I instructed him to go in with a positive mental attitude, and he ended up selling three policies. I took over the next day, and I sold Lopez, Gonzales, and twenty-five others in the main bank in town. Then we sold in store after store, the office buildings, and practically every Spanish and English person we called on, and our manager quickly became a believer!

"The same thing once happened in Rockford, Illinois. A salesman quit and sent in his supplies. He said, 'Nobody can sell in this territory. They're all Swedish, and they're too clannish. They just won't buy.' So I went to the Swedish-American Bank, and I sold policies to the majority of officers and employees. After that, with their support, I sold to the so-called clannish Swedes of Rockford. Another time, I was told that Sioux City, Iowa, was too clannish. Their people's heritage was Highland Dutch, and, what's more, they had had crop failures for five years. I went up there, and we sold every person we called on with a single exception. Furthermore, the one exception that we didn't sell could have been sold, but it would have taken too much time. You see, if it's going to take too long, then I won't waste the time. That's the prospect's time as well as my own.

"I not only believe that every man, woman, and child needs our product, but that it doesn't make any difference where they live. I proved it over and over again. They could live in England, Scotland, Australia—anywhere in the world."

Stone takes a puff on his cigar. "It's really like a game. Naturally, nobody is going to sell everybody. You're going to lose one now and then. But who would want to win every time? It's like playing tennis—you wouldn't want to beat some little kid all the time. You want to have a little competition. When a prospect says no, that's part of the challenge."

One of the difficult challenges that Stone met head-on was the Great Depression. "I didn't realize the actual impact of the market crash in October, 1929, and at first Black Thursday and Black Tuesday were like distant catastrophes that appeared only in the newspapers. I didn't have any money in the market. But instead of buying stocks on margin, I *had* gambled on my own ability to perform. I was taking eighteen hours of credit at Northwestern University, and it was two years before I realized that the market crash was having a serious impact on me and my business. Even many of the smartest men in the nation lost fortunes. But when I realized what was happening, I was $28,000 in debt. My sales force was dwindling, representatives were not producing in volume—I knew it was imperative to quit school and solve my problems. It was necessity that forced me to develop my system referred to above, which I call a *success system that never fails* for those who employ it in its entirety."

Stone decided that the solution was to depend more on his personal production and, at the same time, continue to hire, train, and retrain the agents who were doing a good job. Also, since millions of people were unemployed, he reasoned that his agency could hire selectively. He learned to assess quickly an applicant's character, willingness to learn, and attitudes—positive and negative. He began training agents scientifically. He personally took them out in the field and demonstrated his techniques and selling skills. The sales force received weekly one-page bulletins preaching selling tips, self-motivation, and inspiration, and including a prayer. By 1937 the sales force was back up to 1,000, and today his business career continues an upward spiral.

"If it were not for the Depression," he explains, "I would not have developed the right work habits. I realized that when I was in debt, there was one honorable way of getting out of debt: to make so darn much money that I could pay it off. It's a shame, but most people were just worrying about their problems. I recognized the opportunity to hire huge armies of unemployed salespeople. What's more, we had a proven and successful formula, and we were providing a service which every person needed. During the Depression the demand for our insurance was accentuated."

Stone sums up with one of his favorite quotes: "Every disadvantage can be turned into an advantage." He goes on to philosophize, "It's important to realize that the economy, as well as individual businesses, will move in cycles. Every organism has its cycles; an organism will grow to maturity, level off, and die unless there is new life, new blood, and new activity. When we observe that the rate of growth of any important factor in our company operations—such as sales, profits, or income to our representatives—is leveling off or decreasing, we know that it's imperative to have new life, new blood, new ideas, or new activity.

"For example, we have seen that the income of our salespeople was not keeping pace with inflation. Well, I had to take some kind of action by coming out with new services, increased sales training, and more intensive inspection of their knowledge of self-motivation techniques. Their net earnings jumped tremendously. When salespeople are enjoying prosperity they tend to forget how they got it. They deviate from successful formulas. That is particularly true in the insurance business. Often if they increase their earnings by sales to old customers they stop going after new ones. And that's what had happened. To change the trend it was necessary to motivate them to go back to the original formulas of getting new customers while servicing the old ones.

"Many companies level off and die because management permits sales representatives to deviate from the sales formulas that made the company successful in the first place. When this happens it pays to motivate the sales force to go back to the old systems while keeping pace with new trends.

"A good example is now that we are having inflation, we are solving the problem successfully with new coverages that are very appealing to the public. They cost more and our sales people make more money. Although we make a smaller percentage of profit per unit sold, we develop a higher net profit. So everyone is happy. Even the government is happy!"

Stone has learned how to deal with today's problems from experience with past adversity. For example, in 1939 the Stone organization ran into trouble. At that time he had more than 1,000 agents who operated under his supervision in every state. While Stone and his family were vacationing in Florida, news came that a large Eastern insurance company which the agency represented wished to terminate his services with them. Not only did this mean that every agent's license would be canceled and no policy could be sold or renewed after that date, but the families of his representatives would have no income.

"Now, what do you do when you have a serious personal problem?" he questions. "What do you do when the walls cave in? What do you do when there is no place to turn?

"I told no one. Instead I locked myself in my bedroom for forty-five minutes and turned to God. I reasoned that God is good, right is right, and with every disadvantage there is a greater advantage if one seeks and finds it. I then knelt down and thanked God for my blessings: a healthy body, a healthy mind, a wonderful wife and three wonderful children, and the privilege of living in freedom—in this land of unlimited opportunity. I thanked him for the joy of being alive. I prayed for guidance. And I *believed* that I would receive it."

Stone then made four resolutions: First, he wouldn't be fired. Second, he would organize his own accident- and health-insurance company and by 1956 would have the largest in the United States. Third, he would have net assets in excess of $10 million by 1956. Fourth, he would contact the president of the company that wanted to let him go, regardless of what part of the world he might be in.

"Then I went into action," he relates. "So that my family wouldn't be upset, I went to the nearest phone booth to call the president of the company. As he was a man with principles and understanding, we reached an agreement—our agency had to withdraw only from Texas, due to some difficulties that we had encountered with competitive agents there. A meeting was set up for us at the home office in ninety days."

Since Stone had owned the business, the president agreed to allow his representatives to continue working for Stone with the understanding that when the policies came due for renewal, they could be rewritten through Stone's company, if he organized one, or any company that he chose to represent. Within months Stone obtained complete control of a mutual casualty company in Illinois and purchased the management contract of an assessment company in Texas.

"I converted my 'Positive Mental Attitude' into action," he says matter-of-factly. "And by 1956, although my company was not the largest accident-and-health company in the United States, it was the largest of its kind—the world's largest stock insurance company, writing accident and health policies exclusively."

Stone strongly believes that every individual must set goals. In his book, *Success Through a Positive Mental Attitude*, he stresses four important ingredients to keep in mind when establishing goals:

1. *Write down your goal.* You will then begin to crystallize your thinking.
2. *Give yourself a deadline.* Specify a time for achieving your objective.
3. *Set your standards high.* The higher you set your major goal, the more concentrated your effort to achieve it will be. It will then logically become mandatory for you to at least aim at an intermediate objective as well as an immediate one.
4. *Aim high.* It is a peculiar thing that no more effort is required to aim high in life, to demand prosperity and abundance, than is required to accept misery and poverty.[1]

"Dissatisfied persons change this world," he asserts. "People who reach a certain plateau and quit don't understand that they could accomplish more.

"An individual should always be setting higher goals even before the first are reached. When you see that you are on your way, then you want to see beyond the horizon. In my own case, after having read Lloyd C. Douglas's *The Magnificent Obsession*, I realized that I could develop my own magnificent obsession. It wasn't until recent years that I publicly revealed that all I want to do is to change the world and make it better for this and future generations. Two of the many ways I am bringing this about is sharing with others

[1] W. Clement Stone and Napoleon Hill, *Success Through a Positive Mental Attitude* (Englewood Cliffs, N.J.: Prentice-Hall, 1960).

the concepts of (1) how to recognize, relate, assimilate, and personally apply principles in behavioral sciences, especially in psychology, the functioning of the human mind, and (2) how to apply the Art of Motivation with PMA."

To meet this goal, Stone works through the W. Clement and Jessie V. Stone Foundation, which has given grants in excess of $100 million. The Foundation often motivates organizations seeking funds through setting up a matching fund program. He feels it is important also to train the directors of such organizations on how to raise funds themselves and achieve success through the application of PMA principles. Stone and members of the W. Clement & Jessie V. Stone Foundation have conducted Achievement Motivational Programs in faraway places such as Singapore, Kenya, and Brazil.

Stone's books, *The Success System That Never Fails, Success Through a Positive Mental Attitude,* and *The Other Side of the Mind,* and his magazine, *Success Unlimited,* have carried his success philosophy to millions of people throughout the world. He speaks from experience when he insists that any individual can become wealthy, "no matter how poor his start in life.

"When a new agent comes aboard," he explains, "I believe that the first thing he must do is learn how to set goals. I'll tell him, 'If I had a magic wand and could give you anything in this world that didn't violate the laws of God or the rights of others, what would you want?' I want them to start considering large goals.

"I can remember years ago when I woke up about 2:00 A.M. in a hotel room in McComb, Illinois. I was wondering at the time whether it was worth it to be away from my family. I thought about it for a while and determined the answer was yes, because I could see ahead to the time when my earnings could do many things for my family. I have always believed that it's important to establish big goals in one's life and to make them so worthwhile that one is willing to pay the price, no matter how big a price it may be."

Combined Insurance Company of America is a remarkable organization that reflects its chairman's philosophies. In the 1977 annual report his opening message reads:

PMA—An Important Ingredient of Success. PMA (a Positive Mental Attitude) is a formula that has helped tens of thousands change their world for the better, encouraging them to understand that in adversity there is a seed of an equivalent or greater benefit. A Positive Mental Attitude is the right mental attitude for any given circumstance. It embodies the positive characteristics of integrity, optimism and initiative, in essence the path to a wholesome and successful way of life.

"We have employed persons who've been miserable failures elsewhere," Stone claims, "individuals who were told by psychological tests that they would never make it. And we've made supersalesmen out of them because we know the art of motivation! Unfortunately, at school the individual isn't taught to recognize, relate, assimilate, and apply principles to his personal life. Although he may read a book about someone's success and think, 'Great!' it never occurs to him to ask himself, 'What's the principle?' And when he has the answer, to say, 'That's for me!' We constantly recommend modern inspirational self-help action books to our people. We want them to know how to use the principles and to apply them. I believe that to motivate anyone it is necessary that the goal be desirable, believable, and attainable, or offer the hope of attainment. Hope is the magic ingredient in motivation. And, of course, only the individual can motivate himself. He has to have that inner urge which determines choice or moves him to *action*. To motivate another person, it is desirable for him to know that he is truly an important person. And we'll sometimes have to prove it to him. One effective method with many is to use a statement such as: 'You are one of God's children.'

"There's no question about it," he continues, "we have the jump over all companies that don't help their management understand and practice the art of motivation. It's a continual thing with us.

"We believe that any functioning person can be productive. A few years ago Dr. S. I. Hayakawa and I conducted an experiment. We selected individuals based on only two prerequisites: first, they had to be on relief, and, secondly, they must not have held a job for more than seven continuous weeks in the previous two years. A grant from the W. Clement & Jessie V. Stone Foundation was used to teach San Francisco State College professors the Art of Motivation with PMA. And the professors taught this unemployed group typing, stenography, and other clerical skills as well as how to motivate themselves at will. What happened was completely natural. Over 95 percent of the class got jobs. Four years later, at a class reunion, over 75 percent of that graduating class were with the same companies and many had been promoted. Out of the other 25 percent, some had obtained jobs elsewhere, some of the women had gotten married and were staying home to raise their families.

"It is natural for the disadvantaged to succeed when they are taught *how to* develop and employ the right attitudes, because every living person has a brain and a nervous system— the basis of computer design." Stone keeps repeating, "Until I and a few others got involved, our school systems throughout the world did not train individuals on *how to* recognize, relate, assimilate, and apply principles pertaining to the functioning of the brain and nervous system; specifically: how to tap the power of the subconscious as regards directing one's thoughts, controlling one's emotions, setting goals and achieving them. Or—*how to* develop and maintain a Positive Mental Attitude."

The Combined Insurance Company of America has a sales

force of approximately 5,500 representatives. Under Stone's guidance, it is perhaps the most motivated sales organization in the world. "With a large, international sales force," Stone explains, "not only did we have to have success formulas for our representatives, but we also had to develop additional formulas for management. It's one thing for a salesperson to go out and produce a fantastic record (and we have agents who earn very high incomes), but he may not have paid the price to be a good manager. So we have to teach them how to be effective sales managers. It's my belief that if you set the mind in one direction, you'll get certain results, just as you do with a computer. It then becomes a matter of having another program fed into the individual's own computer. Many of our managers make incomes in excess of $100,000 a year. We take pride in our ability to raise an individual to great heights because he is a thinking individual and can be taught to use what we refer to as 'powers'—both known and unknown."

After a slight pause, Stone rapidly adds, "I also strongly believe that once you feed the right data into the human computer you then must follow up with experience in order to get the right results. Just knowing the theory isn't enough. Take the game of golf, for example. No matter how much you understand the game, you're not going to be able to get up there for the first time and hit that ball well. The subconscious mind needs repetition. It takes practice, practice, practice.

"And we apply the same formula to selling our product as the golf instructor does with his pupil. We teach him the know-how, and then we put him out in the field and let him *sell, sell, sell.* It's the greatest thrill in the world for him to meet people and provide them with a service. The salesperson is having fun. He's laughing all the time, and he's so busy that he doesn't even have time to get out his wallet—he has to put the money in his side pocket! And, boy, let me tell you, nothing succeeds like success!

"I'll tell you something else," Stone continues enthusiastically. "If any man, woman, or youngster wants to acquire wealth, the easiest and surest way to make a fortune is to have some selling experience. Selling doesn't require an individual to have working capital, so it offers an opportunity to acquire financial wealth solely from personal production. The person who works scientifically can make fantastic earnings because, generally, the commissions are structured for mediocrity. And once you know how to sell, you can apply the same principles of selling to any and all vocations. Successful salesmen will prosper in times of boom and during times of recession. And if a depression wipes him out, so what? He can start all over again!"

While Stone was learning the basics of his business career coming up through the selling ranks, he developed an important principle that he has applied as an astute businessman. He calls it OPM, or using *other people's money*. Stone is the personification of an American self-made man. He started with less than $100 in capital and built a multimillion-dollar organization. At the end of 1978 the Combined Insurance Company of America had total assets of $1.02 billion, in excess of $4.8 billion of life insurance in force, and a net income of $77.4 million.

"If you don't have money," Stone booms, "so what? Just use OPM. After all, that's what banks are for. Unfortunately, many businessmen don't realize that and they take loans elsewhere, but it's imperative to develop a good banking relationship. While I don't advise people to go out on the limb with loans, especially when interest rates are high, they should always be very careful about how the rates will fluctuate. And if an individual takes a loan, he should attempt to pay it off in advance. *Never get the bank to agree to loan you money that you can't pay back!* I have always tried to borrow a larger sum than I needed, and I ask for longer periods of time than necessary to pay the money back. By doing this, I can always pay them back before it's due, and I'm protected in case of an emergency."

W. Clement Stone parlayed $100 into one of America's greatest fortunes. He did it by applying his own success formula that he quite willingly has shared with others. "With other people, I am able to multiply my efforts," he proclaims. "But work is fun when you have a high goal and achieve it through hard work. My hours have been 8:00 in the morning until 11:30 at night. When a person has a high goal, he's apt to recognize that which will help him achieve it, and he's willing to pay the price. And he'll continue doing it as long as he has the energy."

Stone practices what he preaches. He generally reads and studies self-help books late into the night. He refers to his reading as his "study, thinking, and planning time." He also enjoys listening to motivational tapes. For extra energy, he sleeps for fifteen to thirty minutes at midday.

Stone has developed a formula for success which applies not only to business, but can be applied by anyone who desires to live a full, rich life. A review of his many nonbusiness activities (included in the biosketch at the beginning of this chapter) illustrates his total involvement in civic and philanthropic activities. "Many people with religious backgrounds give prayers of thanks for their blessings," he says softly, and he recommends that to prove their gratitude, they share their blessings with those who are less fortunate. "It may be sharing part of their wealth, their time, their expertise, or perhaps their philosophies."

Certainly W. Clement Stone has shared his blessings in every tangible and intangible way. Today, driven by his magificent obsession, he is perhaps motivated more intensely than he has ever been. He readily admits that he has a goal that extends far beyond his horizons. He wants to change the world for this and future generations. *And he's doing it.*

MARY HUDSON

3

Mary Hudson

(HUDSON OIL COMPANY)

Mary Hudson is the president and chief executive officer of Hudson Oil Company, the largest independently owned oil company in the United States. She is the first woman in America to have founded an oil company.

The company she founded in Kansas City, Kansas, in 1934 today has more than 300 service stations throughout the country. The privately held corporation's sales volume was approximately $250 million for the year ending December 31, 1978. Recently, *Fortune* magazine estimated Hudson Oil's 1978 profits at $10 million.

Mary became the first woman president of a national oil trade group when she was elected to that position in the Society of Independent Gasoline Marketers of America in 1965, of which she is also a founding member. In 1973 she was a founding member, and is still a member, of the Independent Gasoline Marketers Council. She is a director of the American Petroleum Refiners Association. She is a member of both the Oil Men's Club of Kansas City and the National Petroleum Council, Department of Energy. She is a former director of the Empire State Bank. In 1977 she became the first woman to be admitted to the American Petroleum Institute's Twenty-Five Year Club of the Petroleum Industry.

In 1958 Mary received the Merit Award from the nation of Ecuador. The Desk & Derrick Club of St. Louis, Missouri, named her Out-standing Woman in the Petroleum Industry in 1964. She received the Medal of Honor from Avila College in Kansas City, Missouri, in 1967. She has been an honorary consul to the Republic of Colombia since 1959. Since 1977 she has been a dean of the Consular Corps of Kansas City. She served three terms (1971–4) as president of the Women's Kansas City Association for International Relations and Trade.

Mary serves on the board of governors of the Agricultural Hall of Fame. She is also on the board of governors of the American Royal Association. In 1969 she was on the board of governors for the Baptist Memorial Hospital in Kansas City. She is a member of many local Kansas City groups, including the Kansas City Art Institute (Pa-letteers, Sketch Box); the Kansas City Museum of History and Sci-ence; the Kansas City Philharmonic Association; the Nelson-Atkins Galleries (Society of Fellows); and the Performing Arts Association of Kansas City. In 1978 she was the Special Gifts Chairman of the Mothers' March of Dimes in Kansas City. She is listed in *Who's Who in Finance & Industry,* 21st edition, and *Who's Who in American Women,* 11th edition.

Born in Athens, Texas, Mary has lived in Kansas City since she was seventeen. Her husband, Frank Bane Vandegrift, Sr., died in November 1977. Mary has one daughter, Joyce Cady, who is an executive with the Hudson Oil Company, and two grandchildren, Winslow Hudson Cady and Carolin Hudson Cady.

Mary Hudson, president and chief executive officer of Hudson Oil Company, heads the nation's largest independently owned oil company. She has become an international legend in one of the world's most competitive industries. No other woman in the history of the oil business has achieved comparable success.

While a handful of women have taken over their husbands' interests in oil businesses, Mary's circumstances were very different. In 1933 her first husband, Wayne Driver, was accidentally killed, and the two service stations which the aspiring couple leased had to be given up. At age twenty, the young widow and her six-month-old daughter moved in with her parents.

"About a year passed," the attractive oil executive recalls, "and I became increasingly unhappy about staying at home in my parents' large duplex with my two older brothers and their wives. My money had run out, so I was being supported by my parents and brothers. But I'd had a taste of being independent and having my own money to spend, and I was eager to get back into business and take care of myself.

"My main ambition was to be self-supporting, and the only

thing I knew was the service-station business. Since I had experience in that, leasing a station made more sense for me
than, say, opening a dress store or a beauty shop. Besides, I
liked the outdoor part of the business. As a matter of fact, I'd
still rather be outdoors than sitting behind a desk."

The energetic five-foot-four-inch woman executive pauses
to collect her thoughts. "Everyone advised me not to go into
business. Of course, this was back in 1934, and we were right
in the middle of the Depression, with unemployment around
12 percent. In those days women weren't supposed to work. I
had the feeling that people were thinking, 'It's too bad that
she has to work. Isn't that a shame!' Even the government
was saying, 'Leave the jobs for the men who have families to
support.' Of course, *I* had a family to support too!

"And I never really cared about what other people were
thinking," Mary says decisively. "I just wanted my indepen-
dence. I had too much energy, drive, and aggressiveness to sit
at home, and, besides, by that time I had spent all of my
money! So in the spring of 1934 I borrowed $200 from my fa-
ther and arranged to buy equipment on credit. With the $200
I leased a station in Kansas City. It already had underground
storage tanks, so I only had to install two pumps and an air
compressor. As for staffing it, I hired sixteen-year-old twin
brothers who lived next door to me. They helped clean up and
paint the place, and when we opened they took turns running
a morning and an evening shift. I was in business! I myself
handled the money and bookkeeping. In those days there
weren't many state and federal laws, so the paperwork wasn't
too difficult, and I was able to do it with what I had learned
in high school. When I wasn't doing the paperwork, I'd be
decked out in my white overalls, pumping gas and cleaning
windshields."

Mary remembers being advised by a local businessman,
"Little girl, during the past year this station was opened and
closed twice. Now, if those smart men could not be successful, I'm sure you're going to fail. And you don't look like you

can afford to lose your money at this point in life." She grins as she adds, "He was right about not being able to afford to lose any money, but he was wrong about the rest. I operated that first station for fifteen years, and then the only reason we closed it was for a post-office expansion onto the site."

Mary admits that she gets the same kick out of picking sites for service stations that some women get from rummage sales. In those early days she drove 35,000 miles a year expanding her business.

Within three years the attractive and ambitious entrepreneur had acquired five service stations in Leavenworth, Kansas; Moberly, Missouri; Omaha, Nebraska; and Norfolk, Nebraska. "Leavenworth is thirty miles from Kansas City, Moberly is 120 miles, and Omaha is 220 miles," she explains. "I can remember one well-known station owner advising me, 'Mary, you've got to be crazy! You're not going to be able to survive with so many service stations spread out so far away from Kansas City. It's just too expensive to operate a business that way.' Well, that man's business never grew very large. In fact, one of the main reasons why Hudson Oil was able to survive was that we *didn't* expand just in one place. You see, back in the thirties I witnessed some very severe price wars in Wichita, St. Louis, and Kansas City, and from that I learned never to place all of our stations in one city. If you do and there's a price war, you're not going to make any money for two or three months, and that can ruin you."

Mary recalls a near-disaster with her second station. "In those days the pumps were hand-operated with no meters, so we'd gauge our sales by sticking the tanks. The tanks held 500 to 1,000 gallons, and results could vary by five to ten gallons. If there was a greater variance, something had to be wrong. Well, I was finding shortages in Leavenworth. Since the tanks were above ground, I knew they couldn't be leaking. I changed my attendants and manager, but I was *still* having losses. These shortages were significant enough that if I didn't do something about them, I'd go broke. So I asked an old high-school friend to go to Leavenworth and sit up all night with me to watch the station. I explained to him that since I had checked all of my people so carefully, the answer had to be that somebody was stealing from me during the night.

"We parked the car about a block away from the station and watched. Sure enough, around 2:00 in the morning a small truck drove up. A man jumped out, put a hose in the tank, and started pumping my gasoline out. I quickly called the police and they arrested him."

While some gasoline being siphoned from a Hudson Oil tank doesn't sound earth-shaking today, at the time it determined whether the company would operate at a profit or a loss. This episode also illustrates Mary's determination to do whatever was necessary to overcome adversity. In a field dominated by men, her self-assurance and tenacity have made her victorious where others would have lost hope. She is known in oil circles as a hard-nosed, hard-driving executive whose sharp tongue has forced major-company executives to back down and caused truck drivers to quiver. It's been said that Mary never comes off second best in an argument—no matter who her opponent may be. She knows what she wants, and she has the aggressiveness to go out and get it. She is a supremely self-confident woman who refuses to be beaten.

Mary is also a woman of contrasts. Although always a shrewd, tough, demanding executive, she radiates personal warmth and charm in her civic and social life. Because of her frequent and lavish entertaining, Mary has long been a reigning force in Kansas City society. She is visited by sheiks from oil-producing nations, and has entertained them and as many as 500 other guests in her thirty-nine-room Georgian colonial mansion. Off the job, she reaps the rewards of her hard work and commitment to her career.

"I saw many, many men right here in Kansas City start in the service-station business and eventually get out," she says matter-of-factly. "Operating a service station is not easy. It's

a hard business which takes a twenty-four-hour watch; you're
on call any time, day or night. I've seen so many people quit
simply because they weren't willing to fight it out, to give it
what it demanded. Back in the thirties and forties, it was
nothing for me to get up at 5:00 in the morning and work till
midnight. Hours don't mean anything to me. When you're in
the business world, you just can't afford to think about hours.
That's the worst thing you can do. You've got to think about
the job, and the work has to be done—regardless of the time
it takes!"

Mary strongly believes that getting in at the bottom as she
did is the best way to learn a business. "I literally learned
this business from the ground up," she says, smiling. "In order to supervise the building of service stations, I had to be
able to read blueprints. And I was traveling extensively looking for locations and managing stations. I did all my own
purchasing and marketing. For instance, when I opened the
first stations, I bought gasoline directly from the bulk plants;
however, about two years later I started buying directly from
the refineries. Since there were no pipelines at that time, I
had to buy my own transport to haul fuel out of Oklahoma,
where most of the refineries were.

"I used to be able to build a station in thirty days, and now
it takes a construction foreman about eighty days," she maintains. "Those were trying times because my little girl was
growing up and would cry when I left on my trips. I'd leave
about 6:00 at night to avoid traffic. My mother always ob-
jected, and, being strong-minded, I would tell her, 'Don't
worry. I'll call or someone will if anything should happen.'
But I liked to travel at night and meditate on the next day's
plans."

In the late 1930s Mary joined with her brothers, Murdock,
Tex, and Archie Bob, in a series of partnerships to combine
purchasing and financing for their separate stations, which
they operated independently under the Hudson Oil Company.
In 1968 she and her brothers went their own ways, and they

now compete with one another. The brothers operate their companies under the names Fisca and Highway. "In some places," she comments, "a brother will even have a station right across the street from one of mine."

In 1941 when the United States entered World War II, Mary found herself running all of the Hudson Oil enterprises, nearly 100 service stations. The war years were undoubtedly the toughest of her career. Many independent oil companies did not survive this difficult time. "The government was limiting people to four gallons of gasoline a week," she recalls with a sigh. "Before rationing, our average sale was eight to ten gallons, so that cut our business in half! At one time they only allowed us to sell regular because premium was required for the war effort. Later we were only permitted to be open twelve hours a day, and then the government put in Sunday closings. The regulations changed from time to time, depending upon how much fuel was needed to fight the war, and we had to conform.

"I was losing money, and had to make some very drastic cuts. Some of my top people had to double up on their work. The losses continued for about a year, and then we started to break even. But we never made much money during the war."

Mary sits back behind her black marble-topped desk and clasps her hands. "When the war ended, we just kept expanding," she says. "There's no real difference between running a company with four or five stations and running one with several hundred. Of course, as we grew we'd have larger meetings with more executives attending. But overall we're still dealing with the same type of suppliers, and we use similar equipment. And, naturally, we'd have the same kinds of problems, whether we were small or large."

Although Mary claims that Hudson Oil isn't run much differently now that it has become the largest independent oil company in America, the firm is known throughout the world for its innovative marketing techniques. Not only have Euro-

pean companies approached Hudson Oil to learn its marketing concepts, but the major American oil companies have often followed marketing trends first established by Mary.

"We've always specialized in gasoline," Mary explains,
"and just a few small accessories, such as oil. And we emphasize service. We wash the windshields, check the oil and tires.
We have air at every island. Our stations don't have bays—
we just pump gas. That way, when a customer comes in, our
people are right there in the driveway to serve him. When a
dealer is working inside a bay underneath a car, a customer
has to wait, and when the dealer finally comes out, he's going
to have grease all over his hands. Well, now you're seeing the
majors doing what we've been doing for years. It used to be
that their dealers spent the majority of their time inside, but
more and more of their stations are starting to sell gasoline
only."

Mary pauses briefly and vehemently adds, "The majors always put their service stations on corners, but I don't like corner locations. I prefer the middle of the block; it's more ac-
cessible, so we sell more gasoline. For the same money a
major might spend on 100 front feet at a corner, we could
buy 200 feet in the middle of the block. And it's much easier
to pull into a wide drive than to make a sharp turn at the corner. Well, now you see majors starting to buy middle-of-the-
block locations too, although there was a time when they
wouldn't consider anything but a corner.

"We also elected to spend a lot of money on lighting so the
customer could see the stations well in advance. The majors
used to spend very little on lighting. Another thing we do is
use concrete driveways. Sure, blacktop drives are 50 percent
cheaper, but we put our money into the driveways instead of
the buildings. A large, beautiful building doesn't bring the
customer in. *The money is made on the driveway!"*

Perhaps Hudson Oil's biggest selling feature has been its
ability to charge less for gasoline than the major oil companies do. "We felt that we needed to undersell the majors by

two to three cents a gallon to do the volume we wanted,"
Mary stresses. "It's been very difficult for us to keep it up,
but so far we've been able to. We can do this because we operate differently. The majors have a lot of extra overhead
that we avoid by being small and using good, efficient management. Furthermore, they advertise heavily in the newspapers and magazines, and they spend a lot of advertising dollars on radio and television commercials. They also have the
expense of the credit they extend to their dealers, and of
course they have credit-card expense which we don't have.
All those expenses make for additional cost.

"We've also built a reputation by watching our quality,"
Mary says with obvious pride. "Right from the start, I emphasized that we would sell gas at a lower price, but we always *sell quality*. There was a time when the gasoline wasn't
all the same, and a station could save a quarter to a half cent
a gallon by buying an inferior quality. Some stations operating side by side with us would go out and pick up these bar-
gains. But that backfired on them. Although they made more
profits in the short run, the public soon realized what they
were selling, and their sales really suffered. I suppose it was
just word of mouth that made the public realize that Hudson
Oil means quality, because we didn't advertise. And once the
reporters became aware of it, we started to get some good
publicity. That helped too."

Mary claims that almost the only advertising Hudson Oil
does is in local newspapers for the grand opening of a station.
As a courtesy, Hudson also advertises in oil trade publications. Otherwise, the company relies on its reputation. "And
our price sign is our advertising." Mary smiles.

Evidently her marketing concepts work. The typical Hudson Oil outlet pumps about 100,000 gallons per month; the
average for stations owned by the majors is 30,000 gallons.

When shortages during the 1973 oil crisis closed half of
Hudson Oil's stations, the company began to consider buying
a refinery. After looking at refineries for two years and bid-

ding on three, Mary finally purchased one in 1977 from Midland Cooperative of Minnesota. The refinery, located in Cushing, Oklahoma, cost $20 million, and turns out about 500,000 gallons of gasoline daily, satisfying about half of Hudson Oil's retailing needs. Not only does the Cushing refinery keep Hudson's pumps full, but for every barrel of crude oil it refines, the company gets a rebate of approximately $2 from the U.S. government as part of the entitlements program that aims to keep small refiners competitive with the majors. With this and other cost-saving factors, it boosts earnings by an estimated 25 percent.

With its more than 300 service stations and its own refinery, the Hudson Oil Company has come a long way since the time Mary had to borrow $200 from her parents to get started. And although she may still pump gas at a visit to a station ("It doesn't matter how I'm dressed, it bothers me to see customers waiting, so I go out and wait on them"), her oil business has become world-renowned. Both on business and for pleasure—she has a passion for travel—she has visited 43 countries, her favorites being India, the Arab nations, and crown colony of Hong Kong. She has never had business difficulties in any country because of her sex. "I guess what businessmen anywhere are concerned with," she explains, "is who you are, what your financial statement looks like, and whether you're going to pay your bills or not."

"No matter who I was with," she says, "once we started talking about the oil business, they recognized that I knew the subject. Throughout the world the people I deal with know every important oil company in the United States. And, of course, they're ready to do business with anyone who can make a trade with them and pay the bills. I have always been respected and treated well in the business world, both here and abroad."

Mary pauses to collect her thoughts. "I think the problems of the female in industry have been overstressed," she says softly. "Too many women have become overly agitated, and they're unnecessarily upsetting men. They can get much further in the business world if they don't think about the injustices of the past. Just recently I was asked to sit on a dais at a conference with one of the nation's leading feminists, and I flatly refused. I won't have any part of that kind of thing. I think it's wrong and it benefits no one. I'm for keeping America unified, and I believe those women, while their intentions may be good, are dividing our country. Now, that doesn't mean I'm not for equal opportunity. In fact, we have fifty-four women service-station managers. As managers, women are at least as good as men, and, what's more, they're better housekeepers—and they're more pleasant."

In 1977 Mary became the first woman to be admitted to the American Petroleum Institute's Twenty-Five Year Club of the Petroleum Industry. "Two of my employees were members, but I couldn't get accepted because it was for men only. They had to change the by-laws," she says with satisfaction. "Presently I'm the only woman member, and the way it looks now, it will be years before there's another one."

The Twenty-Five Year Club marks one more first in the remarkable career of this unique and talented woman who thinks like a man in a man's world, yet has a lady's grace and charm.

4

Dale W. Lang

(MEDIA NETWORKS, INC.)

Dale W. Lang is the chairman of the board of Media Networks, Inc., a New York City-based firm that publishes local advertising pages for placement in national magazines. He founded his company in 1968 in Minneapolis.

Dale graduated from the University of Wisconsin in 1955. Following a two-year stint as an enlisted man in the U.S. Army, he began his business career in 1957 when he formed *Select*, a city magazine, in Madison, Wisconsin. In 1959 he founded Select Publications, Inc., which he operated in Minneapolis until 1968. Trade magazines published by Select include *Water Conditioning Sales, Industrial Water Engineering, Feed/Grain Equipment Times, Agricultural Equipment Dealer, Musical Merchandise Review, Linens and Domestics, Wallpaper and Wallcoverings,* and *Twin Citian Magazine,* the nation's first true large-market city magazine. Dale formed Magazine Networks in 1968; in 1972 the company's name was changed to Media Networks, Inc. In January, 1978, Dale himself purchased *Working Woman.*

Dale is actively engaged in a 5,000-head cattle-raising enterprise in Wheeler, Texas. He also competes professionally in Formula Atlantic auto racing.

He was born in Superior, Wisconsin, on June 7, 1933. He and his wife, Joan, live in Woodstock, Vermont. They have three children, Heidi, Eric, and Christopher.

DALE W. LANG

In the world of advertising, magazines tend to be read by people with good incomes and higher education. Naturally this segment of the population is a desirable target for advertisement. However, with the exception of a few city magazines with large circulations, it has never been possible to place an advertisement in a magazine that would pinpoint these potential customers in a given local community.

For example, a Cadillac dealer in Kalamazoo would be foolish to pay national advertising rates for an ad in *Time,* because the magazine has only a 14,000 circulation in the Kalamazoo area. The high cost of short-run printing makes it uneconomical for either the magazine or the advertiser to break down local markets for national publications. Therefore, national magazines, which do reach a high percentage of potential Cadillac buyers, were never an available medium of advertising for *local* Cadillac dealers. The same problem would be true for any other enterprise in the local community—banks, furriers, men's-wear stores, jewelers. Likewise, if a national advertiser wanted to zero in on a local community to test a market or boost local sales, it would not have been able to use national magazines to do the job.

An obvious alternative is the local media, but they are not as effective at reaching the upper-income, higher-educated audience. The number of *potential* customers is the key to effective advertising, not simply large exposure, which often consists of a high percentage of nonprospective buyers. When measured in terms of results, the large-exposure approach can be very costly.

Dale Lang recognized the needs of the local advertiser. To fully understand how he came up with his brilliant concept of "network magazines," one must trace Dale's career back to his college days at the University of Wisconsin in Madison. "I spent my whole working career in the advertising-publishing business," Dale relates. "I worked my way through college by placing posters in all the telephone booths on campus. The poster featured a coed of the week and all of the most frequently called telephone numbers: the sorority and fraternity houses, the dormitories, administrative buildings, movie listings, and whatever else was happening on campus. The local business community purchased ads displayed around the poster. I figured that a phone booth was the only place that a student ever stood still long enough to have the ads hit him. Our ads were outpulling the daily school newspaper by five to one in response."

As a young entrepreneur, Dale was able to pay all his college expenses, and, in addition, he drove away from graduation in a new MG. After graduating he was drafted, but his business continued, operated by students. "My bookkeeper sent me a monthly check, and consequently I was able to live fairly nicely while I was in the service," Dale says with a grin. Upon being discharged, he sold the business.

With his experience, Dale was quickly employed as an advertising salesman for a Madison television station. Then he became advertising manager for an industrial company. "I was so unimpressed there with the salesmen who called on me from trade magazines that I decided I should be in that business," Dale confides. "I believed that what I'd learned about selling consumer advertising would make me very effective in the business publishing field. Trade papers are also an 'easy entry' business. However, before I started a trade magazine, I needed something that would quickly pay the rent, so I started a city magazine in Madison called *Select*. It was one of the first city magazines, and do you know, it's still in existence today!

"It was a controlled-circulation magazine, which is somewhat different than most city magazines today, because ours was not sold at newsstands. We simply isolated an upper-income audience—the country-club members, the Madison Club, the Athletic Club—and we sent the copies to those on a controlled list. Madison isn't that big a town, but we had a circulation of about 10,000. The first merchants I contacted about *Select* were my customers during my college days. The magazine's revenue was generated strictly from the advertising, because we had no paid circulation. I was making a living from it, but I realized that Madison was too small, that I would have to find a larger city for a second magazine. Minneapolis was nearby and didn't have a city magazine. I also knew that Minneapolis was a graphic-art center, whereas Madison was not in the mainstream of magazine publishing."

In 1959, Dale and a partner started *Twin Citian Magazine*, which became one of the first true large-market city magazines in the nation. Simultaneously, the fledgling firm started its first trade magazine catering to the water-softening industry, called *Water Conditioning Sales*.

"There were about 7,000 water-treatment dealers around the country," Dale says, "and every one of them was trying to get business away from his competition. So they would advertise in our magazine. And, likewise, the salt manufacturers, the valve people, and a lot of other product distributors advertised in it."

Now that Dale had his feet wet in the trade-magazine field, he began to launch other magazines. His follow-up magazine was *Industrial Water Engineering*, which was circulated to water users in manufacturing plants who depended heavily on water for their manufacturing processes. Then he started a new product tabloid that went to every firm in the nation that processed or stored grain products. He purchased several other business publications and spent about ten years in the publishing business with city magazines and short-run trade magazines.

Dale's experiences with short-run, low-circulation magazines gave him a thorough grounding in the printing-and-publishing industry and its economics (as compared with long-run printing of large national magazines such as *Time*, which has a four million circulation). His company, Select Publications, Inc. (which later included *Twin Citian Magazine* and eight national trade magazines), rapidly expanded, and although headquartered in Minneapolis, it established a New York office with a staff of editors and sales personnel. The city magazines required Dale to work with national representatives who sold advertising to large national accounts. Following an acquisition of the major representative firm working in the city-magazine field, his company began to sell national advertisements in other city magazines in addition to his own magazines.

"With my experience in city magazines and my strong background in printing, I was well aware of our high production costs on a per-thousand-copies-printed basis," Dale says matter-of-factly. "Our full-color advertising was selling at $60 per thousand due to the poor economics of short-run printing, so our salesmen had to compete with national magazines much lower in cost. For example, *Holiday* was only $13 and *The New Yorker* $12. We were ridiculously high, so a national advertiser would only purchase an ad in one or two city magazines at a time. He would only buy us if he had a particular problem—such as needing to zero in on a given market. Nobody would be willing to pay $60 per thousand to buy all the city magazines across the country when $12 per thousand with a magazine like *The New Yorker* was available.

"That's where I came up with the concept that we could have a magazine network that would produce a four-page advertising section placed in many city magazines across the country. Each of the four pages would have a different national advertiser, and we'd print the four-page section on a very efficient, long-run press with a high circulation of 700,000 copies. By doing that, we were able to dramatically lower the cost of four-color advertising. We initially had fifteen city magazines, our biggest one being *Cue* in New York. By printing 700,000 impressions of a four-page insert, we lowered the cost to the advertiser from $60 per thousand to $15 per thousand! For the first time, it became possible for a national advertiser to enjoy the same economics in local magazines that had formerly been available only in national magazines."

He grins. "We took all of the inefficiency out of it. Even with the $15-per-thousand rate, the magazine publisher was able to enjoy the same profit that he realized with the $60 rate. In effect, even the printer was better off, because the short-run printing wasn't very economical for him either."

With a total circulation equivalent to a 700,000-circulation magazine, Dale's company interested large national accounts that had never used city magazines. The firm landed prestigious accounts such as Old Grand Dad, Chrysler, and Eastern Airlines. Along the way, Dale changed the name of his company from Magazine Networks, Inc., to Media Networks, Inc. (MNI), so he could broaden it to include newspaper supplements and other media in addition to magazines. However, magazines are still the backbone of MNI.

MNI made an important impact on advertising because, for the first time, national companies could advertise economically in local magazines. "It's important to note," Dale points out, "that we were not an ad agency. We were publishers of advertising pages, and we simply sent the pages to the various city magazines for them to bind into their publications."

As Media Networks expanded, Dale gradually sold his trade magazines so that he could fund the network concept. "We were selling off increments; we were building brick by brick," he reflects. "I didn't want to withdraw completely from my other business interests until we were absolutely certain that the network idea would be successful.

"One of our accounts was the Johnson Murphy Shoe Company," Dale notes. "We sold them a four-color page; but they wanted to do it on a cooperative basis whereby they would pay 70 percent and each of their local dealers would pay 30 percent. It would represent a tremendous saving to the local merchant, because he would end up paying only 30 percent of the national rate at $15 per thousand instead of the full $60-per-thousand rate. We decided that by overprinting individual logos of each dealer's name, we could get the efficiency of the long-run press without interruptions. We then had to call on the various dealers in fifteen cities and persuade them to participate.

"Our first call was on Rich's Department Store in Atlanta. We told the buyer that we had great news for him: 'All you have to do is pay 30 percent based on the national rate, and you can have a full-page ad in the *Atlanta Magazine.*' Well, the man thought that it was a great idea, but there was only one problem—he didn't like the shoe that Johnson Murphy was featuring. He didn't think his market would go for that style. He said, 'Use another shoe and I'll buy the program.'

"We encountered a similar problem in Minneapolis," Dale continues. "I went with our salesman to see a large department-store shoe buyer about placing the Johnson Murphy ad in our *Twin Citian Magazine.* I just stood in the background and listened. The man was excited about the program, but he wanted a fur-lined stadium boot in his ad. He was so enthusiastic about the promotion that he said, 'I'll even give you a full window display which will include your magazine along with the shoe.'

"Well, now I was back to zero. If I had to put an individual ad in each city featuring different shoes, I'd be back to the $60-per-thousand cost with short-run printing! It was nerve-racking because there were so many regional differences in the same product line. I can vividly remember standing in front of that big department-store window in Minneapolis thinking how great it would be to have the whole display. But first I had to figure out a way to do it. The question was: How could I get the long-run numbers in Minneapolis? Then it hit me! Even a magazine like *Time* would have the same problem if they wanted to break out an ad in each city, because their circulation in Minneapolis was only 30,000 and my *Twin Citian* was 25,000. So they couldn't do it either!

"But what if I got magazines like *Time, Newsweek,. U.S. News & World Report,* and *Sports Illustrated* to participate in a Minneapolis network? I quickly ran back to the office to do some calculating, and I saw that I could generate about 125,000 circulation in the Twin Cities area if I did that. This was the major breakthrough for our company because we now had a market-by-market program to offer national advertisers as well as the local advertisers. We really had a tremendous selling feature because our only competition for those advertising dollars was the local newspapers, and they didn't appeal to the upper-strata audience that the magazines reached. We decided to package the four magazines and print an eight-page ad section for them in Minneapolis and run the ads one week at a time. For example, the first one in *Time,* and the next week in *Newsweek,* and so on. What a tremendous impact that would have on the reader! In the world of advertising, we don't consider it duplication if it's not all in the same week; we call it *frequency.* We estimated that an advertiser could purchase our twelve-month program and we could deliver virtually 70 to 80 percent of all households with $15,000 incomes and above. That's right, virtually

80 percent of those adults could see that ad a fixed number of times during the year.

"We could now say to the Cadillac dealer, 'Why are you advertising in the newspaper when most people reading it can't even imagine driving a Cadillac, let alone walking in and trying one out? You're wasting a lot of ad impressions. Why don't you advertise to the people who can afford your product?' Well, the local advertiser would say, 'How can I do that?' In the past, with the exception of direct mailings, his only choices were radio, television, and newspapers. Now we could offer him magazines. Suddenly, he could be a selective advertiser! We had a very persuasive story."

In 1968 MNI began to take national magazines and break them into local magazines. Today the company performs this service in more than 150 markets across the nation, and, in addition, is establishing networks in France, Belgium, Switzerland, and the United Kingdom. MNI requires a minimum network circulation of 50,000 and breaks all magazines out according to zip code. The U.S. Postal Department requires all publishers to deliver their magazines in zip-code sequence, which means that MNI simply delivers four- and eight-page inserts to the publishers for binding. Each delivery is broken down into a special market.

It wasn't all smooth sailing. "The difficult part," Dale divulges, "was getting publishers to go to bed with each other; getting *Time* and *Newsweek* to participate was like getting Macy's and Gimbels to lie down together. *Time*'s first reaction was, 'It's a great idea, but don't give it to *Newsweek*.' We had to sell both of them on the fact that we weren't going to be part of the competition they had with each other. That's what they were doing on a national basis. We explained to them that we would take them collectively into competition with local media, and that, for the first time, they would be able to realize local advertising dollars. You see, approximately 50 percent of all advertising is spent at the local level, and the magazine industry had been traditionally forfeiting half the market because they could only compete for national advertising dollars, not spot or local.

"The real significance of what we did was that we *unlocked the local ad dollar for magazines,"* Dale emphasizes. "Just stop and think about that. The other media—television, radio, newspapers, outdoor billboards, and so on—had been able to work both sides of the street, but the national magazines had only worked the national sector. It becomes even more significant when you look at recent studies that reveal the fast pace at which local advertising is growing due to today's sophisticated marketing. So I told the magazines that I was going to go to battle for them against the newspapers, television, and radio and bring them into that local marketplace. What's more, MNI was going to *sell* the advertisements for the magazines. We'd then publish the pages, collect the money, and pay the printers. All they would have to do was bind the pages according to zip codes and bank the monthly check we sent them.

"We finally convinced them to test-market it," Dale continues. "They picked Denver, Colorado. I wanted to do it in Minneapolis because I could telephone my old customers and be sold out in no time at all. But they insisted on Denver, and we agreed to do it their way. We went to Denver, and the results were astounding. We sold eight pages of advertising with twelve-month, noncancelable contracts. It took us only two weeks. I was absolutely amazed."

MNI had become the first media marketing company that published only advertising pages. And it introduced a totally new service to magazines. The company's overriding rule is that it never does anything for a magazine that the magazine can do practically or profitably for itself. (For example, *Newsweek's* circulation in Denver is 25,000, so an advertiser cannot effectively penetrate the market without also using local media to get the job done, and *Newsweek* therefore can-

64   THE ENTREPRENEURS

not profitably offer that service alone.) MNI can offer an advertiser a complete magazine campaign that can fulfill his whole advertising budget.

Dale Lang's network concept has proven so successful that today MNI publishes up to 2,000 ad pages per month, and it projects $45 million in sales for 1979. It is the single largest advertising source for most of its customer magazines. MNI now generates more advertising dollars for *Time, Newsweek,* and *U.S. News & World Report* than does General Motors, the nation's largest company and biggest advertiser. From a profit point of view, advertising dollars of MNI are considerably higher too because they represent a closer net profit, without printing and paper costs to the magazine.

As MNI expanded, its need for additional capital increased. A Wall Street investment banker funded the firm $1 million with equity financing. Ultimately, Dale ended up owning about 60 percent of the company. Rather than having a public offering, the company merged with Minnesota Mining & Manufacturing in 1977. Dale points out, "As a result, we ended up with public stock in exchange for our private stock, so we accomplished the same thing as 'going public.' However, it was a tax-free merger that meant exchanging my stock of MNI for shares of 3M. There's no capital-gains tax to be paid until I sell the 3M stock. I'm really thrilled with 3M because it's such a stable, diversified company."

Today Dale has 190,216 shares of 3M stock, which means that he presently has more than 3M's chairman of the board, the domestic and international presidents, and all nine group vice-presidents combined—thus making him by far the largest stockholder.

With 3M's present dividend paying $2 per share, and at an unearned-income 70-percent tax rate, Dale's latest episode in publishing has been a personal million-dollar investment in *Working Woman,* a magazine which had filed for bankruptcy. "I needed an investment with present losses to offset my dividend income," Dale explains, "but later, when it becomes profitable, I might sell it and realize capital-gains profits. *Working Woman* presently has a 300,000 circulation with a tremendous potential for increasing, since there are more working-age women in the work force today than in the 'non-work force.' And that's for the first time in history. The other women's magazines, like *Ladies' Home Journal, Good Housekeeping,* and *McCall's,* which have 5 to 8 million circulations, are now actually communicating to a minority of non-working women. I think we've got something good going for us."

Conceptually, Dale has visions of advertising to women as a big potential market for sales. "A working woman brings home her own paycheck," he emphasizes. "I don't think her husband is going to pick out her new car. She's going to buy her own wine and liquor. Basically, she'll decide about products that previously were the man's domain. She'll also have independent opinions about where they travel. No longer will advertising in this kind of magazine be restricted to so-called 'women's products.' "

As one of America's most innovative advertising publishers, Dale Lang appears to be on target for great success with this new magazine venture.

5

S. Roger Horchow

(THE HORCHOW COLLECTION)

S. Roger Horchow is president, chief executive officer, and owner of the Horchow Collection, a deluxe mail-order catalog business based in Dallas.

Upon receiving his B.A. from Yale in 1950, Roger enlisted in the Army. Three years later he was discharged as a first lieutenant. He worked for Federated Department Stores from 1953 to 1960, and later spent eight years with Neiman-Marcus, where he was vice-president and group-merchandise director. After a year away in 1968, as president of Design Research in Massachusetts, he returned to Neiman-Marcus as vice-president of the Mail Order Division—the first officer they ever rehired. In 1971 he founded the Kenton Collection and was the president and chief executive officer until 1973, when he bought the company from Kenton Corporation. Its name was then changed to the Horchow Collection.

He has served as a board member of the Dallas Museum of Fine Arts; the Dallas Symphony; Channel 13, Public Broadcasting Company; the Dallas Chapter of the American Heart Association; the American Institute for Public Service; the Hockaday School; and Brookhollow National Bank.

He won the Direct Mail Marketing awards for outstanding catalogs for seven consecutive years (1971 through 1977). Roger was born in Cincinnati, Ohio, on July 3, 1928. He and his wife, Carolyn, have three daughters. They live in Dallas.

S. ROGER HORCHOW

The Horchow Collection is a Johnny-come-lately to the fraternity of brand names associated with excellence. However, in five years it has become synonymous with fine merchandise and ranks in stature with Rolls Royce, Cartier, and Brooks Brothers.

Roger's first hurdle was figuring out what he should rename the Kenton Collection. "We had established an identification during our first two years in business as the Kenton Collection," Roger explains. "According to the contract terms for acquiring the business, I was faced with the dilemma of having to change our name. Boy, we thought of every name under the sun! Finally, somebody suggested the Horchow Collection. (My grandfather's European name was shortened by an immigration officer about a hundred years ago when he came to the United States from Austria.)

"We ran a mailing test with a cooking catalog called the Horchow Collection of Cooks and also sent out another mailing under the Kenton name," the casual, soft-spoken executive explains. "The response was the same, and so we changed the name."

Roger has spent his entire working career in the retail business. He spent seven years at Federated Department Stores, and within eight years he rose from buyer to group-merchandise manager to vice-president at Neiman's. As a merchandising manager he did everything from pricing to promoting the gift galleries, the bridal department, small leather goods, cosmetics, linens, and the bedroom shop. His first experience with mail orders was in 1966 when he worked with the store's so-called "pink sale" catalog. "I knew that there was a tremendous potential in mail order," Roger remarks, "because I watched how our weekly sales figures kept growing and growing."

He left Neiman's and spent a year in the Boston area as president of Design Research, but then while traveling through Dallas to vacation in Mexico he lunched with his former employer, Stanley Marcus. Since Roger had left, Neiman's had been acquired by the Carter-Hawley-Hale chain. To Roger's surprise, Marcus offered him the vice-presidency of the mail-order division. Because Neiman's had a "When you're gone, you're gone" policy with former employees, Roger was astonished by the offer.

He took the job with the understanding that when Stanley's brother, Edward, then chairman of the board, retired in two years, Roger would be in charge. He visualized becoming president of the division. After two years had passed, Roger was told that it might be another three years. "He just wasn't ready to retire," Roger says with a shrug.

No longer wanting to be an understudy, Roger became impatient. He received a call from Robert Kenmore, a former ITT whiz kid who had formed Kenton Corp., a New York conglomerate that had been acquiring "big names" in retailing, including Cartier, Valentino, Ben Kahn, Kenneth Jay Lane, Georg Jensen, Mark Cross, and the Family Bargain Stores. Kenton wanted to start a prestige mail-order catalog, and Roger's credentials looked attractive.

"It was the toughest thing I ever had to do," Roger says, "when I had to say goodbye to Stanley for the second time.

Neiman's let me know that they didn't appreciate having me compete with them in the catalog business. To tell the truth, I hadn't even realized they considered me to be competition."

Roger agreed to join Kenton with the understanding that he would remain in Dallas since "New York is no place to raise my little princesses." Roger's plan was to have a catalog that would sell merchandise from each of Kenton's stores. "Neiman-Marcus always talked about 'everything under one roof,' so I thought it was a good idea for all of these wonderful companies to be under one roof—in a catalog. We named it the Kenton Collection because it was actually a collection of many different stores. The catalog served as an umbrella for a group of merchants."

He points out that the start-up costs of a new catalog are tremendous. In addition to acquiring merchandise, hiring and developing people, and the usual expenses of a new venture, there is the development of a mailing list—by far the most expensive part.

"We began doing business in early 1971. I predicted that we'd lose $1 million during our first year," Roger says matter-of-factly. "I told them that we would break even in our second year, and the third year we'd make $1 million."

Roger's contract provided him with a generous salary that had a slight escalating clause and a share in 10 percent of the pre-tax profits. "The first year, with a $1 million loss, I'd be $100,000 in the hole. The second year, we'd break even, so it would be a washout. In the third year I'd wipe out the first year's losses, and I'd clean up in the fourth year and from then on.

"Well, my first-year predictions held true—we lost a million. Then I hired a friend who talked me into an experiment with magazine advertising. We took two pages from our catalog and put them in many national magazines. My friend knew all the ins and outs about how to work with publishers, so we figured that by advertising in the magazines we would sell enough merchandise to pay for the cost of advertising and in the meantime we'd add a million names to our mailing list. It turned out to be a huge bomb, and we lost another million dollars in our second year on this project.

"Kenton was having troubles and had been taken over by Meshulam Riklis, the Wall Street tycoon and board chairman of Rapid American. Then Kenton had more difficulties, and Riklis started to sell back to their original owners some of the companies that Kenton had acquired. When I saw other people stepping up and buying their companies, I thought to myself, 'Roger, you're a big boy—do it.' I marched myself over to Riklis and said, 'Mr. Riklis, I know you don't think much of my company, but I do, so I want to buy it.' He told me to come back later. That was in late 1972. I went back to him in January and persuaded him to sell me the business for $1 million dollars plus a $500,000 license agreement to be paid out of profits.

"Then I went out to raise $1 million. I found a banker who believed in me. Then I contacted my doctor, my lawyer, and everyone else I knew in Dallas. I told them that they might lose all of their money, but I didn't think they would. A year later I bought many of them out and gave them $25 for every $1 they had originally invested."

Today Roger, his father-in-law, and his brother-in-law own about 70 percent of the business. The remaining stock is owned by Roger's attorney, his controller, and two friends. He admits that he took a big gamble, which included pledging the mortgage on his home.

"I knew from past experience," he explains, "how long it would take to build up a mailing list. I also knew about the costs of merchandise, running a warehouse, and printing a catalog. It was just a matter of time before the orders would fall into place. We projected a 1 percent return on the first million catalogs we mailed out. We got 7,000 orders, which was only .7 of a percent. Then, with the second million catalogs we got .8 of a percent. With our third mailing, our Christmas catalog, we received 44,000 orders. We were on our way." Today the Horchow Collection mailing list consists of 1.4 million names with 950,000 buyers. The company's annual sales volume is about $35 million.

Roger looks back on how his business met with near-disaster when it began to market merchandise in magazines. "It was a horrendous mistake," he admits, "which caused us to lose money rather than breaking even as we were supposed to, based on our second-year projections. However, it did give me the opportunity to acquire the business. I had realized that we'd made a big mistake, but I knew things would eventually turn around. It was just some extraneous activity that caused our setback, and this wouldn't be repeated. The way things turned out, I was very lucky to have somebody else finance all of the start-up costs. Although people thought it would never turn around, I knew that it had to, and—well, it did, didn't it?"

While discount stores were the rage of the 1960s, today's trend is mail order. The mail-order business is said to be a $36 billion to $90 billion industry. Throughout the country, combination discount-catalog businesses have sprung up with catalog showrooms. "Convenience is the important thing," Roger emphasizes, "particularly today with so many working women. We offer everyone a real time-saver.

"One woman gave us our largest-ever order—$20,000 worth of items! She just tore pages out of the catalog and scribbled down that we should send her ten of this item, and twenty of this item, and so on. She broke all of the rules of how a customer is 'supposed' to order from our neat and very simple order blank. But, as I always say, 'I don't care how they buy—as long as they buy.' Of course, I won't mention her name, but I'll tell you this: She's a very rich old lady, and she's also a big customer of many of our competitors."

The clientele of Horchow has included such famous people as Princess Grace of Monaco, Nelson Rockefeller, Barbra Streisand, Robert Redford, and members of the Kennedy clan. Roger admits that he can't tell you everything about his customers, but, according to his mail-order lists, they are *people who buy by mail.* "That's the most important single characteristic that I'm interested in," he insists. "I have people who bring me all kinds of lists of this Junior League or such-and-such country club. But just because people are wealthy doesn't mean that they'll buy by mail from the Horchow Collection. I only know a customer's sex, age, and where he or she lives. Approximately 70 percent of my customers are women between the ages of thirty and fifty-five."

Two years ago the Horchow business acquired a computer that, among other things, sorts out customers so there won't be duplicate names appearing on different lists. Roger states that his company is at the point where it may only net 7,000 names from a rented list of 10,000. "As we grow, we're able to do more and more sophisticated things. When we first started out, I only rented this warehouse, and the business started with practically nothing. We leased all of our outside services, including the art director and our advertising personnel."

When Roger bought his business in 1973, it was his first venture as an independent business person. After working for large organizations for so many years, he suddenly had to make a transition that required him to adjust. He did so very nicely.

"When I worked for a large company," he says with a smile, "there was a standard joke about a 'little black box.' Nobody ever knew what was inside it. In the company, everything seemed very complicated, and there were always a lot of support people to tell me whatever I needed to know. And, of course, there was somebody who was higher up in the organization. But, as I see it, there's really nothing that you can't handle if you put your mind to it. For instance, I'm terrible about fixing things around the house. But the truth is, it just couldn't be that difficult to be a plumber or a carpenter if you really put your mind to it. That's how I feel about my business—if we really put our minds to it, we can make anything work.

"I suppose the biggest change I experienced in making the transition to being self-employed," he reflects, "was how many new things I had to cope with that I had never been exposed to before. My expertise was merchandising. Suddenly, I had to worry about how many cars can park in the parking lot, whether or not we should use styrofoam pellets or foam in our packaging, and a million other details. There were a whole bunch of operational things that had never dawned on me before.

"I didn't have the background in these areas, so I decided that we were going to do everything in the most logical way we could think of. Perhaps the worst reason for doing things a certain way is to say, 'Well, that's the way we always did it.' You'd be surprised how many big companies think that way. When I left Federated and Neiman-Marcus, I said, 'The only thing I'm taking with me is what's up here in my head, and we're going to start all over doing just what makes sense.'

"For example, it had always been a practice when receiving merchandise that the people on the dock never had the purchase order. The poor guy at the dock had to walk a long distance with each arrival of merchandise and get the purchase order from the accounting office. Well, the only reason such a procedure existed was because in the old days there was a lot of wind that could blow the papers around. But in most warehouses today there's simply no reason to do things that way. One of the things we ask ourselves around here is, 'What's the worst thing that can possibly happen?' Well, now our people keep their purchase orders out at the dock, and if one does happen to get lost, we have a photocopy in the office. I suppose that once I owned the company, that kind of attitude was the biggest change we made."

Roger believes that large organizations taught him two important things. "I learned from Federated that 'You're only as good as the people working for you,' and perhaps that's the main reason why Federated is so successful. And at Neiman-Marcus they say, 'Always go for the best.' Well, I guess I'm trying to incorporate those two business philosophies in what we do around here."

Many people claim that the huge success of the Horchow Collection is simply due to the superiority of the catalog. And, of course, the seven Outstanding Catalog awards presented to them attest to the fact that Roger has indeed come up with a better mousetrap. He exercises total control over graphics and passes judgment on every picture that appears in the catalog. He uses fine-coated paper, always printed in full color. He incorporates the best production and printing techniques. All merchandise is displayed in realistic, sophisticated settings. Often he will use his own family and home. Seeing a Clovis Ruffin nightgown on a store rack doesn't compare to viewing it in a Horchow issue on one of New York's top models. The plush graphics are the catalog's trademark and they present a look of elegance beyond compare. The holiday issue alone costs more than $1 million to produce. And every page of it will have its readers desiring the "good life" that it portrays.

Although names like Cartier, Georg Jensen, Geoffrey Beene, Tiffany, and Baccarat are prevalent throughout the catalog, Roger insists that "we only use a brand-name product if it means something to the consumer. For instance, if I happen to pick up something from China or perhaps Germany on a buying trip and the name doesn't mean anything to our customer, we won't have a name on it in our catalog. We also do not follow the common practice of using cooperative advertising money from manufacturers. We want to be in absolute control of our own destiny. We don't want to feel obligated to anybody because they contributed toward the catalog production. They may try to dictate to you about what should be in the catalog and how we should do their page. That just creates an unnecessary interference."

A shrewd merchant, Roger clearly understands what his customers will buy. While the mail-order business may look easy, Roger warns that it's a highly specialized industry. He cautions that there are enormous risks in purchasing merchandise that you must inventory without knowing what will actually sell. "Unlike a retail business," he stresses, "we cannot buy in small quantities. We must purchase large quantities of single items."

In selecting a product for the catalog, the prime question Roger and his associates ask is, "Would I buy this product for myself?" Also, "Would my wife, my mother-in-law, or somebody I know want it?" Of course, there are other considerations to be reviewed pertaining to the value it represents and, naturally, how profitable it would be. Originality is also a factor, and in addition the Horchow organization is interested in how well the item will photograph—will it be easily understood in a catalog? Because all merchandise is shipped to the customer, the packaging and shipping are also factors.

"Since our conception," Roger emphasizes, "we have not deviated from our general merchandising philosophy. We have experimented in new areas, widened our assortments, but the original concept remains the same: to present fresh, useful, and interesting merchandise of good value, at any price level, to an audience of prosperous customers. The definition of *prosperous* is left to the customer, since our merchandise prices vary from $5 to $10,000. There should always be something for everyone!"

One of the Horchow Collection's best-selling items was a small savings bank. The top all-time best-seller is a $12 set of glass plates and bowls which, Roger believes, conform to standards of beauty, economy, and practicality. Of course, the Horchow Collection has had its share of losers too. "I had always considered myself an expert on children's clothes," Roger drawls. "After all, I do have three daughters. So I was very excited about the wonderful purchase of 500 black velvet dresses from a famous London dressmaker. The only problem was that the dress was not styled for the American child, and, furthermore, I placed it in our January catalog. My wife, Carolyn, informed me that American girls don't wear a velvet dress after Christmas. We still have 500 dresses!"

Many people are curious about how the overhead of a mail-order business compares to the expenses of the conventional retailer. "Although we have a greater selling cost due to our catalog and mailings," Roger explains, "our other overhead is lower because we're in a low-rent district and we don't employ nearly as many people. We have only 250 employees. However, we have 500 people during peak seasons, most notably at Christmas. When you break it down to the bottom line, we'll end up with a similar after-tax profit, about 5 percent."

Usually the Horchow Collection takes thirty-two pages, though the Christmas catalog runs sixty-four pages. Roger believes that a lengthy catalog bores readers. Rather than having a bigger catalog, he has two others called *Trifles* and *Pfeifer*. The Horchow Collection comes out at the beginning of every month, and *Trifles*, which offers a little less fantasy and less fantastic prices, is available in the middle of each month. *Pfeifer*, which incidentally is his wife's maiden name, has three issues a year and offers traditional men's apparel. "Why shouldn't we have three catalogs?" Roger asks. "Since everybody else is competing with us, we may as well compete with ourselves!"

Another enterprise has emerged from the Horchow Collection. Called L'Envoi (The Sending), it is their first fragrance venture. An ounce of L'Envoi retails for $75 and a quarter ounce for $27. A two-ounce spray cologne costs $13.50. Roger's idea for L'Envoi is that it will gradually gain recognition and he'll add a product, such as talc, soap, bath oil, and lotions, per catalog. Eventually he'll also have a men's cologne. As initial orders are processed, it appears that L'Envoi will be a huge success. And, according to recent sales of its Horchow Label Products to noncustomers (based on the recognition of the Horchow name), the prospects of franchising the name to manufacturers in ready-to-wear and other product areas appear feasible.

Who knows, perhaps someday a Horchow product will appear in the Neiman-Marcus catalog!

6

William J. Richards

(RICHARDS FARMS, INC.)

William J. Richards is president of Richards Farms, Inc., in Circleville, Ohio. The current farm operation consists of 6,000 acres: 2,000 acres in corn, 2,800 acres in soybeans, and 200 acres in wheat, with the balance in hay and pasture. It also has a 250-head cow-beef herd and extensive grain-handling and storage facilities.

Bill owns a 50 percent interest in Circle S. Grazing Association (458 acres) and is its secretary-treasurer. He has a 50 percent interest in Richards-Scherer, a 1,000-acre farm partnership, and a 25 percent interest in Loch Leven Farms, a 7,000-acre farm partnership in Mississippi. He serves on the board of Robinson Hybrids and Ploughshare Partners, and is the past president and current treasurer of Premium Agricultural Commodities, Inc. He is also the president of Agri-Business Consultants, Inc., located in Columbus, Ohio.

In 1966 he was named Ohio's Outstanding Young Farmer by the Ohio Jaycees. The U.S. Jaycees honored him in 1967 as Outstanding Young Farmer of America. He has served as secretary-treasurer, president, and chairman of the board for the National Outstanding Farmers' Association. He is a founder and past president of Ohio Top Farmers. Boards he has served on include those of the National Farm Foundation (Chicago), Top Farmers of America (Milwaukee), and the Ohio Cattlemen's Association.

His many speaking engagements include addressing the National Policy Conference of the United States Department of Agriculture in 1978; the National Agriculture Building Conferences in Florida (1977); the National Livestock Producers in Kansas City (1977); and the Harvard Agri-Business Seminars (1975). In 1977 he worked with CBS-TV on a special report on the use of agricultural pesticides that was featured on *60 minutes*. He was the first farmer program participant at the U.S. Department of Agriculture's Outlook Conference in Washington, D.C., in 1976, and the same year he addressed the National Fertilizer Institute in Cincinnati. He also participated in the Agricultural Engineers' Conference at Chicago (1974), the No-Till Conference in Honolulu (1974), the Agronomy Farm Science Days at Michigan State (1971, 1972) and Purdue (1971–2, 1978–9), and the Purdue Top Farmer Computer Workshop (1970, 1972, 1974).

Bill is a member of Ohio State University's Presidents' Club. Currently, he is president of Ohio State University's Agriculture Alumni Association. He has served on review committees of the USDA, including the Economics Committee (1977), the Engineering Committee (1976), and the Agronomy Committee (1975). Since 1968 he has been on various county and state committees of the Republican Party. He also takes part in many local civic activities.

Bill was born in Richmondale, Ohio, on October, 19, 1931. He received a B.S. degree in agriculture economics in 1953 from Ohio State University and took graduate courses there in 1954, 1964, and 1965. Bill and his wife, Grace, have three sons, Steve, Bruce, and Elmon. They live in Circleville, Ohio.

Although Bill Richards has a rural background, unlike many present-day owners of large farm holdings, he did not grow up on a farm. "My father had a farm-implement business," he explains, "and growing up in an agricultural community gave me a lot of exposure to farming. I decided that I wanted to go into farming, and majored in agriculture at Ohio State University and later studied agriculture economics in graduate school.

"In 1954, while I was in graduate school, my wife, Grace, and I bought a farm near her folks for something like $140 an acre. It was a 325-acre farm owned by a farmer who had really let it run down. From the looks of it, he must have been a trash collector!"

Both Bill's and Grace's parents signed down-payment notes for $20,000, and the young couple financed another $25,000. Bill continued to work on a part-time basis at the farm-implement store of his father, E. E. Richards. "I guess the biggest help I got from my family was their moral support," he says, "and some old, used equipment I borrowed from my dad's implement lot. In addition to working at the store, my wife and I wanted to open a gravel pit, since at the time less than half our land was usable and we had only about 100 to 150 acres of crops. We had to bulldoze and clear trees for the pit, so this borrowed equipment got us started in the gravel business. That business generated badly needed extra cash. Then in 1955, just one year after I started on my own, my father retired. We wanted to buy his business, but we were just too young to tackle it along with the farm."

Bill often lectures to Ohio State agriculture students. One of the most common claims he hears about farming is that it's much more difficult getting into the business today than when he started. The students believe that the high cost of land and equipment makes farming prohibitive for a young person starting out without substantial funds. "I guess everyone likes to look back and say, 'It was easier in the old days,'" Bill says with a grin. "Of course, that's an argument young people made when I was getting out of school, but I didn't buy it then, and I don't today. I do believe that technology in agriculture is changing so fast that the well-educated person today has a real advantage over his grandfather. All his grandfather had was his labor and whatever money he could pull together.

"There's so much innovative technology available," Bill continues, "and this, I believe, is a tremendous advantage to the student who comes into the business today with an open mind. In the past five years a major change has come about in agri-colleges as people have realized the high potential profit in farming. As a result, the universities are swamped with city kids. As a matter of fact, for the first time there are more students from the city than from the farm. Now so many people think that if you major in agriculture, you must become a self-employed farmer. Well, that's simply not any more true than that the student who graduates from business college will automatically start his own automotive company. Just as he is more likely to be employed by an automotive company than to own one, there are many agricultural careers other than owning your own farm. There are many

WILLIAM J. RICHARDS

farming jobs comparable to those in industry, and with similar responsibilities, and I think they're more interesting than their counterparts in industry."

Bill claims that he can't think of any business where he would have had as much growth potential as in farming. "Sure, the return on investment was low during the fifties when I first started. But that's typical of any business during the early years. You know, a statement I take great exception to is, 'Farming is a way of life.' I've been very outspoken about this because *farming is a business like any other business.* Now, that's not to say that I haven't had a very good life. However, like anything else, farming has its pros and cons. I don't have the privacy of my counterpart in a city business. I can't get away from the job like a city businessman, because I can't go home at night. And this business will absorb all the money we can generate. There's always a place in my business for any excess funds. Of course, in my opinion, that's an advantage. I don't have to look for investments like a lot of business and professional people do."

Recently Bill, with three partners, bought Loch Leven, a 7,000-acre plantation in Mississippi. When Loch Leven was purchased it was a pecan-grove and cattle operation, but the new owners immediately began to upgrade it into more profitable soybeans. "Now that we've turned it around," Bill says with satisfaction, "we have an attractive opportunity to sell it. You see, I think of that land as just another commodity, and if the price is right, I'm in favor of selling."

He looks thoughtful. "Now, a lot of farmers get upset about this kind of thinking. For example, two years ago I sold some land to a group of foreign buyers and then rented it back from them. This caused quite a stir with some of the farmers in the community. They acted as if I had handed something sacred to a bunch of foreigners. I'm afraid that public opinion right now favors legislation that shuts off foreign investors. I think that's a serious mistake.

"I believe that one of the things that's going to determine

the success of the American farmer during the next few years is our government's trade policies," Bill continues. "This country can't afford to become more protective and place restrictions on foreign trade. The agriculture industry is more dependent than any other industry on foreign trade because we have such an excess capacity here. We're capable of moving 30 to 50 percent of our production to other nations. Any restriction, even a simple restriction such as keeping foreigners from investing in our land, is not good. We really have to have a flow of money both ways, going out and coming in. As I said earlier, we have to think of land and farm products in the same terms as any other commodity."

Bill is also outspoken on the subject of energy. "Some people think the high price of energy will hurt the farmer, but I believe that, in the long run, it's bullish for agriculture. Every time oil goes up, my land becomes more valuable, because it's an energy producer, a giant solar collector, gathering the sun's rays and turning them into valuable food. Also, when energy becomes more expensive in other areas where it is needed for irrigation, my land becomes more valuable, because it gets free water in the form of rain. So, part of the increased value of farmland during the past few years is directly related to the increase in the cost of energy. Another bullish factor: in order to keep those trade dollars balanced and make up for our imported oil, this country has to export more wheat, soybeans, and other agricultural products."

Bill was a member of an agriculture group that recently traveled to Australia and South America to study other countries' farming techniques. About the trip he states, "I am absolutely convinced that there's a tremendous agricultural potential in the world. The world can certainly feed itself with its present population, and perhaps even with twice its present population. I believe that the food shortage in this world is political, not physical. We're really not scratching the surface of what we're capable of producing."

Bill pauses to reflect. "You take that great big corn belt,

the American Midwest. That big hunk of land is the very best in the entire world. You know, people can do an awful lot of arguing about what made this country great. They give credit to us being innovative and highly motivated. And that's true. They also give credit to our free-enterprise system, and that's true too. But don't ever forget that huge breadbasket out there. It may have been the most important thing of all. It's our system working with that land which made it all work.

"Another thing," he adds with conviction, "you hear a lot of people complaining about the government's role in our business. Well, our society has progressed to the point where the government plays a role in *every* business. The agricultural industry takes the strongest stand about getting the government out of its way. But can this country and we farmers really afford the luxury of that freedom? You must keep in mind that food supplies have to be as constant as possible, regardless of a boom or bust in agriculture.

"I truly believe that our government's land-grant system has played a tremendous role in developing and supporting the farming industry. I have the highest respect for the United States Department of Agriculture. The USDA provides free research and a free flow of information among farmers, and I feel that's the biggest asset a firm of our size has in competing with the big money coming in and controlling the agriculture industry. As long as this free data is available, this country won't see giant corporations taking over the independent farm operator. Of course, when you talk about price controls, we want the minimum of government control.

"I spend a lot of my time collecting information about agriculture," Bill continues. "I'm constantly attending seminars and schools. I've taken numerous short courses at Ohio State and Purdue, and I went to the Harvard Business School for its Agri-Business Executive Education Program in 1974, 1975, 1976, and 1979. Changes in technology are happening so rapidly that it's essential to stay on top of the field. It's also useful to meet with agri-business leaders."

Bill is currently president of a co-op which consists of ten Ohio farmers. In addition to realizing a definite economic advantage in buying and marketing its farm products, the group meets once a month to exchange ideas. Each member has specialized in a certain area, thereby enabling all members to realize maximum benefits from the organization. One of the group serves as a fertilizer chairman, one as a seed chairman, and another as chemical chairman. Bill believes that this trading of talent and information has been invaluable to his farming operations.

"I've been blessed with the opportunity to receive a good education in agriculture, and fortunately I was able to apply it when I started farming," he states. "Perhaps one of the things that made our growth so rapid in the early days of my career was our minimum-tillage program. I've received some credit for my innovative technique of cutting down the trips over the field. This technique has certainly minimized expenses and made us very competitive with our neighbors. Actually, I had an advantage when I got out of college in not having farm experience—it meant that I wasn't bound by traditional ways of doing things. I just couldn't see the purpose of plowing and disking, dragging and cultivating, and going through all these steps, as most farmers do, to produce corn. I decided to skip the intermediate steps and go over the field just once to plant it and a second time to harvest it. Well, we proved that we could do it this way. It saved fuel and labor, and we put the savings into acquiring more land. We were able to plant an acre of corn in twelve minutes, while it was taking other farmers an hour. Another thing I tried, and it worked, was growing corn and soybeans on every acre, at a time when most people thought that you had to rotate your crops and keep cows, pigs, and chickens and everything else. We just skipped all of those steps.

"Later we were among the first to use agricultural chemicals—mostly weed chemicals, that is. This, too, let us farm a lot more acres with the same amount of equipment and labor. Also, I always believed in using the largest equipment available for a job. At one time my twenty-four-row corn-planter was one of only four in the nation. I had the manufacturer of a sixteen-row make up a twenty-four-row for us. Its capacity is simply amazing. It will do forty acres an hour; that's 400 plus a day, sixty feet at a sweep. And we can fill it with enough seed to plant 140 acres of corn without stopping!

"I have always been willing to try new concepts in farming," Bill adds, "and I believe it's essential to think of farming in the same terms as any other business. One of my wisest business decisions in this regard was going to Columbus for my banking needs. It wasn't as though I was having a particular problem with the local banks, but I discovered an entirely different banking atmosphere at a large, national bank in a major city. I told the Columbus banker that I didn't want him to treat me as a farmer, but as a businessman. Well, he ended up giving me even more credit than I asked for; I didn't need it, but it was great for my confidence! While it was traditional when borrowing money in agriculture for the local bank to put a mortgage on everything, the Columbus banker wanted only my personal signature. He said, 'I wouldn't know what to do with those cows if you fail and we have to take them back.'"

Today, Bill says, many people approach him to invest money in his farms. "There's plenty of capital available from willing investors," he asserts. "But a shortage of capital is not the problem. The only limiting factor on our farms is my time and my ability to gain control of land. Now we have one son who recently graduated from college and two more who graduate within a year. While it would be nice for them to work somewhere else for a year or two to get some outside experience, we can't afford the time. We just need more people here, and the boys want to be part of the business. I would have to say that the biggest challenge I face during the next five years is bringing our sons into this business and having them become successful. It's difficult to pass a large farm operation on to the next generation. It would be much easier for me to hire management than to have our sons come into it."

Bill Richards seems to have a handle on everything at Richards Farms, and if his sons are anything like their father, the family business will be in good hands for future generations.

7

Gary Goranson

(TIDY CAR INC.)

Gary Goranson is the founder and president of Tidy Car, Inc., a company that specializes in appearance maintenance of automobiles. He founded the company in early 1976. Now headquartered in Mississauga, Ontario, Tidy Car has more than 2,000 associate dealers located in twenty-seven countries, including the United States, Canada, Puerto Rico, Trinidad, Curacao, the Philippines, Aruba, Germany, Norway, Australia, Belgium, New Zealand, Malaysia, Saudi Arabia, Kuwait, Tahiti, Israel, Indonesia, Guam, and the Virgin Islands. It is the largest company of its kind in the world.

Gary was born in Ottawa, Ontario, on April 2, 1942. He and his wife, Camille, live in Toronto. They have one daughter, Rae Louise.

GARY GORANSON

A high-school dropout ("Who would ever hire a guy with only one eye and eleven years of formal education?" he quips), Gary briefly attended a secretarial school in Saskatchewan in 1960. Upon reading a "sales opportunity" ad, he quit secretarial school and began selling fire alarms door to door. Six months later he started selling vacuum sweepers; he spent the next ten years representing several sweeper distributors throughout the United States and Canada. His earnings fluctuated during these years ("In 1966 I earned $90,000 at age twenty-four, and in 1969 I could barely pay the $15-per-week rent on our trailer in Erie, Pennsylvania"). In 1970 Gary claims to have built up another sales organization which was one of the largest vacuum-sweeper distributorships in North America. Again, in 1971, he met with a disaster when prospects of new Canadian legislation caused many finance companies to discontinue the practice of discounting conditional sales contracts for certain in-home sales organizations. ("In the late sixties I experienced the same catastrophe in Chicago," Gary adds.) Later in 1971 he decided he'd lost interest in the door-to-door selling and, with a partner, he opened a Magnavox television store in Toronto.

By 1972 it was the largest Magnavox dealership in Canada (with a sales volume of $1,600,000) and one of the company's largest in North America. He then became a regional manager for Magnavox for almost two years.

"For the first time in my career," Gary explains, "my wife and I thought that we had some security—but it was a feeling that didn't last very long.

"In November, 1975, the company was taken over by North American Philips, and I, along with all other Magnavox employees, were told that our services would no longer be needed. You see, with Canada having a total population of about 20 million, Philips didn't want to compete with Magnavox in such a small market. I found myself without a job.

"Since there had been rumors spreading that Magnavox would cease merchandising its products in Canada, I had already been thinking about going into business for myself."

He confesses that the Tidy Car idea first entered his mind the previous May when his wife started talking about needing a new car. "Camille had a 1971 Meteor. We'd taken care of it mechanically, and since she'd only put about 6,000 miles on it each year, we anticipated getting a good trade-in price.

"Unfortunately, we never paid too much attention to its appearance. When we took it to the dealers, they expressed little interest in a car that looked like it had been driven through a war zone. We were told that car shoppers don't bother to look under the hood of an auto with a poor appearance. You see, most of us think that if we keep a car in good mechanical shape, that will be sufficient. But if the car doesn't look appealing on the lot, the customer will never get close enough to examine the engine!"

Gary ended up getting $100 for his wife's five-year-old car; better-looking cars of the same vintage were going for $1,500.

"That's where I got the idea that people must take better care of their cars' appearance," he says. "When I investigated, I found out that it costs $75 to $150 a year for a profes-

GARY GORANSON 97

sional wax-and-polish job in order to keep a car looking like new. At the same time, I concluded that one of the reasons why I never took my car to the shop was the inconvenience. I'm a real son-of-a-gun when it comes to taking my car in even for an oil change. I just don't have the time to go there, wait, and then come back in a few hours and wait again! That's where I began thinking about the mobile aspect of Tidy Car—we'd go to the customer's location. Just think of the convenience we'd offer our customer!"

While trying to plan for his future after he left Magnavox, Gary found out at the age of thirty-four that he was diabetic.

"While in the hospital," Gary recalls, "I reread a favorite book of mine, *Think and Grow Rich*. Boy, I needed all the positive thinking I could get! I needed that rest in the hospital to put things together. I was really excited about starting Tidy Car when I got out.

"But my friends, relatives, and everybody else kept telling me I was nuts to take a gamble and go into business for myself," Gary remembers. "They advised me to get a $20,000-a-year job and be satisfied. Then I read an excerpt from a book called *Total Commitment* about Kemmons Wilson, the founder and chairman of the board of Holiday Inns. Wilson said, 'In the time it would take for me to find someone willing to pay me $25,000 a year salary, I could make $100,000!' Well, that really struck home because that's exactly how I felt! Right then and there I decided to take the plunge."

Undaunted by the fact that he would face unemployment upon being discharged from the hospital, he immediately began to formulate his plans for starting Tidy Car.

"I suppose that most people would have been thinking about why they *shouldn't* go into the business." Gary tosses back his head and laughs. "Considering my track record of failures in the vacuum-sweeper business, I should have thought about that too. But I was determined that this time I had a winner, that I was really on to something big! In retrospect, I suppose I have always been a highly motivated individual. Perhaps much of my motivation is compensation for self-consciousness about losing the sight of one eye in an early-childhood accident. I guess a psychologist would say that I had to prove I wasn't handicapped."

During his convalescence Gary put his entire plan down on paper. He began thinking about his various options for financing. "I had been unemployed for a couple of months, and, well, you just don't accumulate very much money when you've been working for somebody else," he confides. "I took my ideas to my banker. Although she was skeptical, I showed determination and enthusiasm. So, while I didn't get the $10,000 I was asking for, I did get $5,000, and that money put me in business!"

By January, 1976, Tidy Car had become a reality. Gary's first major step forward was when he was quickly able to locate a manufacturer of a special buffing machine. "I found a company that manufactured an 'orbital' unit whereas most units operate in a circular fashion," he explains. "A rotary buffer creates a tremendous amount of heat from its spinning disk and often causes damage to the painted surface by burning, marring, or gouging. Even a professional using a rotary buffer can accidentally damage a car.

"Our special equipment was originally developed for aircraft. Believe it or not, at one time it was common practice to actually hand-polish every part of an airplane. In fact, even today every part of a 747 is polished before it is assembled."

Gary claims that, although Tidy Car's first few months were very difficult, the company actually made money. "As you can see, my $5,000 wouldn't go very far, and I wasn't able to purchase much merchandise. As quickly as I was able to generate some cash, I had to put it right back into the business to buy additional equipment and supplies to pay for more advertising, and to pay my two employees. My main object was to equip operators and get them out into the field. I realized that Tidy Car was a wonderful opportunity for thousands of people to go into business for themselves with a very small investment in materials and supplies. By late 1976 we were ready to test our franchise program in Toronto.

"I decided to present the opportunity for a franchise to some of the individuals who had been working with me on a piecework basis during our first months in business, and some of them took the offer."

The Tidy Car services (including exterior polishing, vinyl roof revitalizing, and interior shampooing) were well received by car owners in the Toronto community. Gary decided that he should advertise Tidy Car as an opportunity. "In early 1977 we placed an ad in the *Globe & Mail* newspaper. The *Globe & Mail* has national distribution throughout Canada, so we began to receive inquiries from all over the country.

"The idea caught on like wildfire!" Gary exclaims. "Within two months the new enterprise had 100 dealers; within a year there were more than 500. By 1979 we had more than 2,000, and we're now doing business all over the world. What's more, we're just getting started!"

It costs less than $1,000 to become a Tidy Car franchise representative, and that small investment provides enough chemical supplies to generate approximately $3,000 worth of business. "Since the average job costs the customer between $60 and $80, the operator earns $20 to $30 an hour," Gary explains. "Tidy Car offers one of those rare opportunities— an individual can invest less than $1,000 and actually be in business for himself. Some of our dealers are earning more than $1,000 a month part-time. That's perhaps the main reason why our business has taken off like it has. Tidy Car is a good deal for the car owner, the associate dealer is prospering, and the company is generating a nice profit."

Labor is the most expensive part of the Tidy Car service. An associate dealer will spend about 7 to 9 percent of revenue for materials, and he also pays Tidy Car a $2 royalty for each job.

"Now that we're getting to be a large company, we're incorporating sophisticated systems to keep track of our operators and our operations," Gary states. "In the beginning we operated strictly on the honor system in collecting the royalties. To some extent we still do. However, through the marvels of the computer age we're able to keep close tabs on each operator's activities, and we know his exact production. We analyze computer print-outs for each dealer on a weekly basis so we can have current 'activity information' on each territory.

"In addition, some of our services involve warranties which Tidy Car stands behind, but we'll only guarantee a job when we receive the warranty card. The dealer must submit it along with the customer invoice, and a copy is left with the customer for him to forward to us. The warranty registration card contains the dealer's operation number for identification purposes.

"We also carry liability insurance that protects our Canadian dealers against any claim arising out of the use of the chemicals. In the event that the dealer did not initially send us a customer invoice at the time of the job, he risks having the insurance company deny the claim."

Gary quickly smiles. "Of course, we don't expect our customers to have the paint come off their cars. We give the best cleaning-and-polishing maintenance job in the business. But in this day and age a business has to be covered by liability insurance, and our group rate is far less expensive than what a dealer can purchase on his own."

Gary points out that Tidy Car is selling a concept, not a magic buffing machine and chemicals. "We have a program, and if the dealer follows our system, he's going to succeed," Gary stresses. "We even have a 115-page manual that includes everything from advertising for customers to recruiting workers. We have regional meetings throughout the year. And, boy, I can't emphasize strongly enough how important it is for us to establish effective communications with our people. We're constantly on the telephone with them. And we have a monthly newsletter called *Tidyings* that is absolutely essential to our success. The newsletter is full of new ideas; most important, it gives production figures of the leading associate dealers throughout the organization. When other dealers read about the high earnings realized by the individuals who are willing to get out and really work, they know that they can do it too.

"It's very important for our independent dealers to know that they're part of an organization," Gary adds. "We're offering continual assistance. I mean, anyone can open a hamburger stand, but thousands of investors want the one with the golden arches out front."

Many of Tidy Car's successful dealers are enterprising individuals who hire several part-time and full-time workers. The dealer then is free to handle advertising and promotion.

"This is a labor-intensive business requiring only a small investment," Gary asserts. "The cost of the supplies and equipment in our business is a very small percentage of the service we perform. And because the cost of Tidy Car is mainly labor, in countries where the cost of living is low the cost of labor for our services will be correspondingly low. It's all relative."

There are presently more than 2,000 Tidy Car dealers, of whom approximately 70 percent are located in the United States. Gary projects thousands more during the 1980s. He believes that the potential market on a worldwide basis is phenomenal.

"Wherever there are automobiles, airplanes, boats, or any other product that needs our service," Gary confidently declares, "Tidy Car will be there to do the job."

MARY KAY ASH

8

Mary Kay Ash

(MARY KAY COSMETICS, INC.)

Mary Kay Ash is the founder and chairman of the board of Mary Kay Cosmetics, Inc., a Dallas-based company. On December 31, 1978, the company had more than 45,000 independent Beauty Consultants, and the total net sales for the year were $54 million.

Mary Kay began her sales career with Stanley Home Products and represented the direct-sales party-plan company for thirteen years. Later she joined World Gift, a company selling decorative accessories in the home, and was eventually named their national training director. In 1963, with the help of her son, she started Mary Kay Cosmetics. The firm had grown large enough by 1968 to become an over-the-counter, publicly held company. In August, 1976, its stock was listed on the New York Stock Exchange. In 1978 the company had a net income of $4.8 million.

Mary Kay individually and the Mary Kay Foundation, which she founded in 1968, have donated monies to countless charitable organizations in the fields of religion, education, the arts, and health; many have come to depend on this support. A few of these are the Dallas Civic Opera, the National Foundation for Cancer Research, St. Mary's University (Myra Stafford Pryor Chair of Free Enterprise), and the Society for Prevention of Cruelty to Animals.

In 1976 *Business Week* listed Mary Kay as one of America's Top

100 Corporate Women. In 1973 she received the Marketing Citizen-
ship Award of the Memphis Chapter of the American Marketing Association. She was awarded a Horatio Alger Award in 1978, when
she was also named Cosmetic Career Woman of the Year. The
same year she was presented the Dale Carnegie Leadership Award.
In 1979 she was the subject of a *60 Minutes* television profile. Many
cities and states throughout America have named her an honorary
citizen. She has been keynote speaker for numerous groups and associations.

Born in Hot Wells, Texas, she has two sons and one daughter.
She and her husband, Mel, live in Dallas, Texas.

In 1963 Mary Kay Ash invested her life savings in a new cosmetics business venture with her husband. They recruited nine salespeople. One month to the day before the doors were to open, Mary Kay's husband died of a heart attack. Mary Kay was told by her attorney that she must liquidate the business and recoup whatever cash she could or she would be left without a cent. Her accountant advised her that the commissions she was prepared to pay her sales force would make it impossible for her to succeed and it would be just a matter of time before she was bankrupt. Mary Kay listened very carefully. Then she did exactly what she thought was best, and the company opened for business on schedule, September 13, 1963, with nine saleswomen.

"I saw the world collapsing around me," she says. "But when God closes a door, He always opens a window."

Through the new opening entered her twenty-year-old son Richard, who decided that he could run the financial and administrative end of the fledgling company. He accepted a $250-a-month salary, half as much as his guaranteed earnings as an insurance agent had been. Mary Kay was then able to concentrate on what she did best: selling, recruiting, and training.

"Aerodynamics has proven that the bumblebee cannot fly," Mary Kay recounts the old adage. "The body is too heavy, and the wings are too weak. But the bumblebee doesn't know that, and so it goes right on flying." Appropriately, the symbol of Mary Kay Cosmetics is the bumblebee. "Without a doubt, my biggest thrill in this business," she emphasizes, "is seeing women have their own personal dreams fulfilled in a career. So many women don't know how great they really are, that they really can fly! They come to us all *Vogue* on the outside—and vague on the inside. In the beginning, many women just have no confidence at all."

It has been said that Mary Kay doesn't simply recruit a sales force or sell products as much as she transforms personal lives. Some people have described her as a "born-again cosmetics salesperson." A deeply religious Baptist, she admonishes her 45,000 independent saleswomen that they must keep their lives in the proper perspective—"God first, family second, and career third."

It's not uncommon to hear a Mary Kay Consultant say something like, "When I started working for Mary Kay, I was too shy and introverted to speak in front of two people. Now I think nothing of addressing a convention of 8,000."

The attractive, petite chairman softly drawls, "A woman usually comes into our organization as a tight little rosebud, sometimes appearing at my door too timid to even tell me who she is. Then I watch her after six months of praise and encouragement and she's hardly recognizable as the same person."

Perhaps it was Mary Kay's mother who most shaped the philosophy that Mary Kay now passes on every year to thousands of women throughout the world. Mary Kay's father was an invalid, and her mother managed a restaurant in Houston from 6:00 A.M. to 9:00 P.M. "Mother was never home. In the morning I went to school, and when I got home I fixed the meals and cleaned the house. At age seven, I was already taking the streetcar into downtown Houston to buy my own clothes. I really had a hard time convincing the sales clerks to sell me anything. Whenever I needed my mother, I could phone her and she would say to me, 'Honey, you can do it.'

"My mother gave me a priceless gift," Mary Kay reminisces. "She would always tell me, 'Honey, you can do anything you want to do if you want it badly enough and you are willing to pay the price.' Now that's exactly what I tell my Consultants—that they can do it, too."

With this type of personal incentive, Mary Kay made straight A's through school. With no money for college, she got married. Her husband was drafted in World War II, and she found herself raising their three children alone. When he came home, he told her that he wanted a divorce. "That was the lowest point in my life," Mary Kay recalls. "I felt like a complete failure as a woman."

With three children to support, she didn't have time to feel sorry for herself, so she became a dealer for Stanley Home Products. The job appealed to her because she was able to work and fulfill her duties as a mother. As a salesperson, she did not start off setting the world on fire. She knew that there was a great deal to learn, so when she was invited to the company's sales convention in Dallas, she borrowed the $12 it would take to pay for her transportation and hotel. A friend lent her the money, but suggested that she ought to be spending it on shoes for her children, rather than going to conventions like men. At the convention, because she had no money for meals, she ate cheese and crackers in her room.

During the convention one woman was crowned "Queen of Sales." At that moment Mary Kay vowed that she was going to be Queen the following year. She gathered up enough courage to tell the company president about her ambitions. "Mr. Beveridge took my hand," Mary Kay says, "and looked me square in the eye and said solemnly, 'Somehow I think you will.' Those five words changed my life. Somebody believed in me!"

Mary Kay went on to become a leading salesperson for the Stanley Home Products Company. Later she worked for another direct-sales organization. Eventually she became that company's national training director at a salary of $25,000. "Actually I was really acting as sales manager," she explains, a bit chagrined. "Several times I would take a man out on the road for training, and after I'd been teaching him the business for six months he'd come back to Dallas and end up being my superior at twice my salary. It always irked me when I was told that the men 'had families to support,' so they deserved more pay, because I had a family to support too! It seemed that a woman's brains were worth only fifty cents on the dollar in a male-run corporation. And what was most upsetting was being told, 'Mary Kay, you're thinking like a woman.' "

In 1963 Mary Kay decided to retire. "I quickly discovered why they put in the obituaries, 'He retired last year.' I really believe that sometimes when you retire from your life's work, you retire from life too," Mary Kay explains. "I think many people die out of sheer boredom. Well, that was the most miserable month of my life. Formerly I had not had enough hours in the day; that month I didn't have any reason to get out of bed. In order to keep busy, I began writing my memoirs. Then I decided to write a book about selling for women. I felt that my twenty-five years' experience should not be wasted. Perhaps I could help other women over some hurdles I had encountered. In order to organize my thoughts, I started to write down all the good points of the companies I had worked for. Then, after two weeks, I listed the things that I felt should have been different. In preparation for beginning the book, I read all my notes and the thought struck me, 'Wouldn't it be wonderful if somebody started a company like this instead of just talking about it?' I decided to put my money where my mouth was. I decided to do something about this fantastic company I had written about. I was going to give women opportunities I had been denied."

Mary Kay's first step was to buy the skin-care formulas from a woman she had met in 1953 at a Stanley Home Products party. She describes their meeting: "The woman was hostess for a Stanley party with about twenty women attending, where ages varied from nineteen to seventy. I was demonstrating the Stanley products, and I kept looking at these women who had such peaches-and-cream complexions. At first I thought it was the lighting in the room. Every one of them had such beautiful skin! After the Stanley party, we all assembled in the kitchen for coffee, and the hostess started passing out little white jars with black tops to everyone except me. As she handed them out, she would make notations in a little book and say, 'Now, let's see, you have used the number three for two weeks, now use number four for seventeen days.' She would then hand them a little jar.

"They all looked so great," Mary Kay laughs, "I admit I wanted a jar too. I became somewhat upset when she looked at me and said, 'You have aging skin. You could really use some of this. I'd like to use you as one of my guinea pigs.' She handed me a shoebox with some skin freshener and night cream in an old bottle that still had a prescription label on it! Also in the box was a direction sheet with terrible grammar and incorrect spelling.

"I was a little dubious, but the women around me kept saying, 'Don't worry, honey, you should have seen me six months ago. I looked worse than you.' These women looked great now. I thought to myself, 'She really does have these people brainwashed!'

"It took me a full twenty-four hours to convince myself that I should try it. Finally, I gave myself a facial. My ten-year-old son, Richard, came in after school and gave me an 'I'm home' kiss. He turned around in the doorway and said, 'Gee, Mom, you feel smooth.' I thought to myself, 'It's just not possible to get results from *one* facial'—but my face did feel wonderful.

"When I retired, I had been using the product for ten

years, so I knew how well it worked. My mother had also used it, and when she died at age eighty-seven, the nursing-home people couldn't believe her age. She looked like she was in her sixties.

"It was a formula that this woman had received from her father, who had been a hide tanner. He had noticed that his hands looked much younger than his face, and the only possible reason was because of the tanning solutions he worked with every day, so he began using it on his face. As a result, when he died at age seventy-three, he had the skin of a much younger man. While he had proved his point, no woman would ever do what he had done, for the process was time-consuming, obnoxious, and smelly.

"While everyone else ridiculed him, his daughter supported his concepts. She moved to Dallas to become a cosmetologist and worked seventeen years to develop creams and lotions that women would use. She had no idea about how to market them, and she finally gave up hope of ever distributing them on a large-scale basis. I bought the formulas from her, and this transaction was the basis for the 'dream company' I planned to build."

Mary Kay was "sold" on her product because she knew personally it worked. Today she is a great-grandmother, but she certainly doesn't look it. How old is she? "A woman who will tell her age," Mary Kay says with a smile, "will tell anything."

At first, Mary Kay had a local cosmetics firm manufacture her product. Having a marketing background, she knew exactly how she wanted to package and merchandise it. Today Mary Kay Cosmetics houses research and development and production facilities in a modern 235,000-square-foot plant located next door to its corporate headquarters in Dallas. Here the products are formulated, processed, and packaged before being transported to five regional centers for distribution. The Mary Kay line includes skin- and hair-care products, makeup, lip and eye colors, fragrances, plus a line of skin-care products and toiletries for men. The company is proud of its superior products, and it realizes that the principal reason why women join their ranks is because they themselves enjoy using Mary Kay Cosmetics.

One of the reasons Mary Kay Cosmetics is special is its consultation services. Unlike other sales organizations that often christen their representatives *consultants* to avoid the word *salespeople*, Mary Kay Cosmetics professionally trains its consultants to demonstrate skin-care and makeup techniques. While door-to-door cosmetic companies simply take orders, and retail stores' clerks sell products over the counter with little or no instruction, Mary Kay offers two hours of skin care and personalized guidance.

The Mary Kay employee's mission isn't just to sell, but to teach good skin care. Unlike other direct-sales organizations (at Mary Kay Cosmetics it's referred to as *person-to-person consultation*), her business offers a "Beauty Show" to an audience of four to six participants. The show is an adaption of a marketing concept Mary Kay learned from Stanley Home Products. She believes that women feel more relaxed when they're in a group, and she emphasizes that sales-pressure techniques are taboo in her organization. A Beauty Show generally lasts two hours.

"We teach skin care," Mary Kay explains. "The average woman doesn't know how to take care of her skin. She has usually bought a jar of something from a department store and a jar of something else from a drugstore, and she has no routine whatsoever. She mixes up different chemicals from this company and that company without realizing the adverse effect of such chemicals in combination. So not only does our program give them a perfect skin, but it also educates them on how to keep it."

A high percentage of company representatives are women who became interested at a Beauty Show. "It's an amazing thing," Mary Kay reveals in a gentle voice, "how many women come to a show with an 'I'm-not-going-to-buy-a-thing' attitude. Sometimes they say, 'There's nothing you can do for me—I was born this way!' Oftentimes we have to coax and cajole them, and then they sit down and begin to get involved. In about an hour or so, you can't pry the mirror from their hands. It's just amazing! Before you know it, they're asking, 'How can I become a Consultant?' "

One of Mary Kay's favorite sayings is, "There are three ways to get word out fast: telephone, telegraph, and tell a woman." She shakes her head and laughs, "I can't explain it, but something can start in New England and by nightfall be in California. It's the fastest network of communications in the world." Simple enough, but that's how the Mary Kay Cosmetics phenomenon has spread not only throughout the United States but also to Canada and Australia.

There are no assigned territories. A Mary Kay Consultant is free to sell when she is on vacation or wherever her husband may be transferred by his company. Likewise, a woman can recruit other salespeople anywhere. "If a Consultant is vacationing in Hawaii," Mary Kay says, "she can recruit a Consultant, give her initial training, and then leave her in the hands of a Director there who will contrive to provide guidance and inspiration. She will draw a small percentage of her recruit's wholesale purchases. But it's important to remember that the company pays that commission, not the recruit.

"The Hawaiian Director does not get a percentage; however, she may well have a recruit in someone else's area, so it balances out. We have over 900 Sales Directors and nearly all of them have 'adoptees' in their units.

"Men don't usually understand our system," Mary Kay says, smiling, "but it works! Everyone helps everyone else." It's no wonder that Mary Kay Cosmetics has been described as a vast sorority.

Mary Kay Cosmetics does not sell franchises or distributorships. Advancement cannot be bought; it must be earned. Nor should the company be confused with a "multilevel" sales organization. All products are sold directly to the Consultants, who, in turn, sell them to their customers. Field management consists of independent Sales Directors, Senior Sales Directors, and National Sales Directors. When a Beauty Consultant meets certain standards in selling and recruiting, she is eligible to qualify as a Sales Director after a training program. As a Sales Director, she assumes responsibility for the continual training, motivation, and guidance of a Sales Unit, which consists of her recruits and their recruits. A Sales Director becomes a Senior Director when one of her recruits forms her own unit. A Senior Director becomes a National Sales Director by developing ten or more Offspring Units. There are approximately 900 Sales Directors and sixteen National Sales Directors. The average annual income for a National Sales Director is $56,000.

Each recruit pays $65 for a Beauty Kit. All orders to the company are paid for in money orders or cashier's checks. Because Mary Kay has witnessed many direct-sales companies go broke due to loose credit policies, she does not permit even her oldest and most successful salespeople to send in personal checks. All sales representatives pay their own expenses when they come to Dallas for a week's training program in management. "There's really a commitment when they have to pay their own way to Dallas," Mary Kay asserts. "When a woman has an investment in her traveling and lodging costs, I can guarantee you that she'll work twelve hours a day during her visit. There's no monkey business—she'll take notes, and after classes she'll study every evening."

Similarly, every representative pays her own way to the annual Mary Kay convention in Dallas. More than 7,500 Beauty Consultants attended the 1978 convention, which was held in the Dallas Convention Center. The company spent more than $1 million on the extravagant three-day sales seminar.

In addition to teaching its representatives about beauty care, the convention will inspire the sales organization to achieve even better results in the following year. Dozens of women are called on stage to receive expensive gifts (mink coats, gold and diamond jewelry, trips to Acapulco, and the use of new pale-pink Cadillacs and Buicks). It's common to hear representatives make comments like, "I'm going to go home and sell everything that moves—wait until next year!"

The pink Cadillac has become a status symbol among Mary Kay people because it signifies superior performance. "We award the use of a pink Cadillac for one year," Mary Kay states, "and if a representative doesn't produce the following year, she must give it up. 'Nothing wilts faster than a laurel rested upon.' And, I'll tell you, it's awfully hard to go back to driving a black Ford once you've driven a pink Cadillac. People really notice a pink Cadillac. When you drive it up to an intersection, they're going to let you through. *The waters part!*"

Mary Kay believes in motivating her huge sales force, and giving praise is one of the most effective ways to do this. Each week she personally signs about 2,000 letters that offer encouragement. "Likewise, when I make a criticism, I always sandwich it in between two layers of praise. Women can't take criticism," she explains. "If a man comes home from work and says to his wife, 'Where did you get that dress, Goodwill?' he just blew $100, 'cause she'll never wear it again.

"We're constantly praising our representatives," Mary Kay continues, "and the round of applause that our new people receive when they do a good job is probably the first applause they've ever had."

Obviously, a combination of good product, motivation, and praise is the right formula for success. But while praise and applause are appealing, they can only go so far. It's tremendous income opportunities that inspire and maintain sales forces. As Mary Kay sums it up, "My greatest sense of accomplishment is the unparalleled opportunity that we have provided so many women. Nothing excites me more."

9

Joseph Sugarman

(JS&A GROUP, INC.)

Joe Sugarman is the president and sole stockholder of JS&A Group, Inc., headquartered in Northbrook, Illinois.

JS&A was founded by Joe in 1971—in the basement of his home. Today the company is America's largest single source of space-age products, with sales approaching $50 million. Joe is nationally known for his innovative advertising techniques. During the year he conducts a seminar at his estate in northern Wisconsin where participants pay $2,000 to spend five days learning his advertising and marketing concepts. A popular and entertaining public speaker, Joe has given his inspirational speech "Five Steps to Success" to audiences throughout the United States and Canada. In 1979 Joe was chosen Direct Marketing Man of the Year.

Joe was a civilian agent in the U.S. Army from 1962 to 1965. He then worked in the CIA as a special agent. In 1965 he was co-owner of Ski Lift International, and the same year founded JS&A Advertising. In 1971 this was changed to JS&A National Sales Group. He founded JS&A Group, Inc., in 1974.

He majored in electrical engineering at the University of Miami in Florida. He lived in Germany for four years, and speaks fluent German. An instrument-rated pilot, he has multi-engine and commercial licenses. He has been an amateur radio operator for twenty-two years, and is an avid skin diver, snowmobiler, water skier, and jogger. He is also an award-winning photographer and writer.

Joe was born in Chicago on April 25, 1938. He and his wife, Wendy, live in Northbrook, Illinois. They have two daughters, April and Jill.

After high school Joe Sugarman wanted to study journalism at the University of Illinois, but his father wanted him to study electrical engineering and Joe enrolled at the University of Miami in Florida as an electrical-engineering student.

Although Joe proved to have a strong aptitude for engineering, his taste for journalism continued. "Actually," he recalls, "ever since I was three years old, I was attracted to advertising. I can remember my father reading the newspaper and saying, 'Hey, look at this ad,' and, sure enough, even before I could actually read, I began looking at ads."

It all jelled one day when he was eating ribs in an off-campus restaurant and the owner peevishly inquired, "Say, kid, do ya got any ideas how I could get the students to come to my place?"

"Well, I suppose you could advertise in the school newspaper," Joe offered.

"Whadya think I should say?" asked the restaurant proprietor.

"Well, whatever you say, it has to be different," Joe nonchalantly replied.

At this point in the story a big grin breaks out on Joe's

bearded face. "The deal was that I'd get free meals for a week for my services," he explains. "The following Friday I walked into the restaurant, and the place was packed. The owner came running over to me and said, 'Joe, I don't know how ya did it, but the kids are just flocking in here. Ya gotta write ads for me every week.'

"Well, after a few weeks of eating greasy ribs and chicken, I decided that I'd branch out. Before long I was working for a clothing store, a bookstore, an ice-cream parlor, and several other restaurants. I became the best-fed, best-dressed guy on campus," Joe laughs.

He had one semester left to earn his degree in electrical engineering. But during the Berlin crisis he was drafted and ended up in Germany with Army intelligence. He then joined the Central Intelligence Agency for about six months. He left the CIA after meeting some ski-lift manufacturers in Switzerland who wanted to do business in the United States. Joe handled the promotion and sales for the ski-lift company and a partner handled the engineering.

"Every time we sold a ski lift, the resort owner asked if we could help them with their promotion; they were very impressed with the job we were doing for the ski-lift company," Joe recalls. He ended up with three ski-resort owners as clients and resigned his position with the ski-lift company to form an advertising agency. His small business included some political accounts, a few restaurants, and his three ski resorts.

"I ran my ad agency for about six years," Joe explains, "and I was always on the lookout for something whereby I would someday strike it rich. Boy, did I have my share of failures! They provided me with a real education. During the Batman craze I came up with a brainstorm of printing up Batman credit cards. I approached the New York people who had exclusive Batman rights, and they were so excited over the idea, they wanted to go into business with me. After I had 250,000 credit cards printed, I contacted the company. Following weeks of waiting to hear from them, finally I was

JOSEPH SUGARMAN

informed that the president of the company didn't like the idea.

"I was absolutely sure that my idea was a winner, and I visualized making millions overnight. Then, out of the clear blue sky, my whole dream was destroyed.

"That was just one of my incredibly big disappointments," Joe continues. "There were other times I felt so sure that I was about to become a millionaire that I started reading the classified ads for mansions and picked up brochures on Cadillacs. Then in the next moment I would totally lose the dream. I would be back to zero and have to start all over again. Thank God I was able to bounce back."

In 1971 Joe read about a small pocket calculator that used a new integrated circuit. After $26 worth of phone calls, he convinced the calculator company that he could market the product by direct mail. When Joe presented his idea to his client, a direct-mail company, he was asked, "Who would want to buy a $240 item through the mail? Especially a calculator that nobody ever heard of." Still convinced that his idea was solid, he told the manufacturer that he could market the product himself.

Joe recalls, "I got some of my friends together and raised $12,000. I agreed to double their investment before I'd take a penny of profit for myself. After that, I would own the business, and any additional profits would be mine. I could have invested the whole $12,000 myself, but if I had failed, we'd have been back to TV dinners and struggling with the mortgage on our new home.

"I selected eight different mailing lists—you know, engineers, accountants, etc. My list broker added two more: presidents of million-dollar corporations and presidents of $100 million corporations. Each list had 5,000 names, and I sent out the 50,000 mailings. I only needed .2 of one percent to generate a profit, so I was absolutely convinced that I couldn't fail. Most mailings generate about 2 percent. However, I ended up with only .1 of a percent response, and we lost half of our money.

"Well, in the process, some very interesting things developed," Joe says with a slight smile. "First, I found that two of the lists made money—the two presidents lists. Second, the calculator manufacturer had dropped the retail price from $240 to $179. I went back to my investors and showed them that if we concentrated on the right lists, along with stressing the reduced retail price, we were certain to make money. I then explained that I was willing to take my personal money and invest it in the new mailing, and if they were willing to stay in, it wouldn't require an additional investment. They agreed to go along with me; we sold a ton of calculators. They doubled their money, and I then owned my own company."

It was later, when it was rumored that the price of calculators was going to drop, that Joe had to act fast. Since direct mail was a time-consuming process, he decided to advertise in the *Wall Street Journal.* Within two weeks after the ad appeared, Joe had made a $20,000 profit.

Joe Sugarman has since become a legend in the booming mail-order business, which by some estimates is a $75 billion industry. The prestigious industry newsletter *The Mail Order Analyst* recently stated that since 1972 JS&A probably has offered more innovative micro-electronic products than any retailer, mail-order firm, or single manufacturer. Products of JS&A include electronic burglar alarms, mini-calculators, computer scales, digital watches, computer games, and a complete array of space-age products. Joe has become the guru of the industry. Currently he conducts four five-day mail-order seminars each year at his Wisconsin estate. Although his tuition is $2,000, he generates enough response from a single ad to fill up three classes of sixteen participants each.

When Joe first started advertising in the *Wall Street Journal,* he ran big display ads because, as he puts it, "I wanted to build confidence in the consumer's mind and I wanted people to think that my company was big. Actually, for the first couple of years we were very small. We operated out of my basement. I can recall businessmen coming to the house to pick up a calculator. The baby would be screaming in the background and my wife would answer the door saying, 'You want JS&A? Go down to the basement.' Wendy was very understanding and gave me her complete support. But naturally the business became an infringement on her privacy, so when we were ready, we moved to some nearby office space."

Joe also recalls that his secretary came to work for him on a part-time basis from 9:00 to 3:00. "But we got so busy that Ms. Stanke ended up working until 3:00 in the morning," Joe laughs. Today she is an executive vice-president of JS&A.

JS&A has come a long way since those early days. Today the firm has plush offices and warehousing in Northbrook, northwest of Chicago. Joe is a big believer in using the most efficient equipment available—a strategy which keeps his labor costs down. He has had as many as fifteen WATS lines manned by fifteen talented phone operators, and he uses some of the latest, most sophisticated computers. Joe's love for technology evidently goes beyond the merchandise that JS&A sells.

"I carefully select for my largely upper-income male clientele an array of toys that look nice and do all sorts of nice things," says the space-age executive when describing how he continually comes up with winners. "I'm a connoisseur of gadgets. Or perhaps I'm just a guy who has good taste."

A close study of his merchandising techniques reveals expert marketing combined with outstanding timing. For example, Joe was offered a small walkie-talkie at the start of the CB radio craze. "Instead of using the walkie-talkie idea," he says, "I focused on the CB angle and called the product the 'Pocket CB.' We've sold more than 250,000 of them during the past three years."

With jogging an "in" thing, JS&A now offers a $150 Japanese-made jogging computer with digital read-out. It consists of a platform on which the jogger runs in place. Its sleek console measures the pace and distance of his run.

"I look for products that are faster, cheaper, or somehow better than existing items," he explains. When he came out with the Canon P10D calculator, which simultaneously prints the computation on paper, its novel printing head made the machine lighter, smaller, and cheaper than other models. "As soon as I saw it, I knew that it was better than existing models, and that I could show people why."

Although Joe is continually approached by hundreds of manufacturers and inventors, fewer than 10 percent of the calls and letters he receives are worth even a look. He knows that he can't sell just anything, and much of his success is his ability to narrow down his choices to a selected few. "Many of these so-called inventions are simply gimmicks," he asserts. "For instance, I won't sell the calculator pen because I think it consists of a lousy calculator and a lousy pen. I feel the same way about the pocket TV sets. They aren't really pocket-size, so I'll just wait until they get smaller. Many of these items I refer to as 'multifunction products.' "

Joe admits that he has made some selections that even *he* couldn't market. "I had a 'Mickey Math,'" he recalls, "which was a Mickey Mouse calculator. I thought it was going to be the next pet rock. Well, a calculator is a serious product, and I believe that the Mickey Math didn't sell because people wouldn't buy it as a joke.

"Then there was my $1,500 laser-beam mousetrap." Joe winces. "I thought if you built a better mousetrap, the world would beat a path to your door. Well, I had one that would detect a mouse with a laser beam, then would activate a spring-loaded wire trap. It was a beauty—mounted on a polished walnut base that could blend in with the decor of any plush executive's office." Although his ad described the trap in detail, the better-mousetrap adage apparently didn't apply; not a single one was sold.

His biggest financial flop was a $250,000 loss on a "checkbook with a brain." It was a $40 electronic device that recorded savings deposits, checking balances, and virtually every banking transaction. "People would rather write such information in their checkbooks by hand," he surmises.

Although some of Joe's failures have resulted from his defiance of the proven rules of the mail-order and advertising industry, this strategy has also provided him with unprecedented success. A favorite "Sugarmanism" is: "A successful person learns all the rules and follows them to the letter; a supersuccessful person learns all the rules and then breaks them, one by one."

Supersuccessful Joe has indeed broken the rules of advertising and then revised them to suit his own whims. His ads look much like the editorial format of many publications. *Popular Science* and *Mechanix Illustrated* are particularly effective for JS&A ads because the stories and ads seem almost interchangeable. The ads give important messages about specific "new space-age technology breakthroughs" that are the "latest developments" in their field. For a relatively modest breakthrough Joe's ad might be 500 words or so; for a major breakthrough an ad might be 1,400 words. His 3,000-word ads are themselves a revolutionary breakthrough. In them he reports technological products and scientific progress. His ads sometimes extol progressive individual competitors and entire industries.

However, despite his writing ability, Joe considers himself a salesman rather than an ad man. "There's so many things that you have to do in selling; you can't do it with very little copy," he explains. "Sure, perhaps some products don't have to be sold, and with little copy you simply act as an order taker. On the other hand, I have taken products that nobody else in the country is moving, and with good copy I'll sell tons of them. It's like a salesman who tries to sell a prospect in two minutes, and another salesman takes thirty minutes to give his presentation. Well, in thirty minutes you'll convince a person—that's the difference between a short ad and a long one."

He adds seriously, "In order to succeed in this business, you must understand your market. The key is knowing how to sell your product. Don't for a moment think it doesn't involve salesmanship. A good ad will get results, a poor one will fail. It's just like the good salesman compared to a poor salesman—even though they're both selling the same product."

What's more, Joe's ads never have a coupon. He admits that even if a coupon pulled a bit better, he would continue with a no-coupon ad because he wants an editorial look.

JS&A was the first mail-order company in America to use a WATS line. Joe claims that most of his business comes by telephone orders. His phone operators always ask if a customer wants the deluxe model and specific accessories that ultimately increase the dollar purchase of the customer.

While most mail-order companies have what's referred to as the "back end," an offer to sell a customer another product when an order is fulfilled, JS&A has never made such an offer. "We treat our customers royally," Joe states. "Consequently, during 1974, when most mail-order businesses were in trouble, our business continued to grow. While we don't offer them anything to buy when we ship an order, we do offer them other products in our catalog." Today the JS&A catalog accounts for nearly 50 percent of the company's total sales.

Most advertisers think that the same ad will generate higher results when repeated over and over. "It just doesn't make sense," Joe asserts. "You must have a gap in between with magazine ads. Repetition might be applicable, in radio advertising, but in my business the law of diminishing returns is bound to occur. Repetition only pays off when the same ad appears in many publications at the same time. The public will think, 'It must be really selling; it must be a good product.' I guess the key in selling is 'belonging.' People want to belong to the group of people who own that specific product. They want to belong and identify with the crowd that buys it."

An estimated 60 million people are reached by JS&A ads. That's a lot of people, and Joe Sugarman wants them all to belong to "his" crowd. Many of them already do.

10

Richard D. Schultz

(NATIONAL REVENUE CORPORATION)

Richard D. Schultz, founder and president of National Revenue Corporation, is also the chairman and sole stockholder. Founded in 1973, the cash-flow management services firm is now the largest company of its kind in the world. Based in Columbus, Ohio, it has offices in major cities throughout the United States. Wholly owned subsidiaries include American Creditors Association, American Creditors Collection Bureau, Management Evolutions, The Inkwell Printing Company, MediAd, Borror & Associates, National Revenue Insurance Services, Inc., and Manchester Life Insurance Company.

Richard belongs to the American Society of Association Executives. He is vice-president of an independent, nonpolitical, fact-finding organization of the Executive Committee of Citizens Research, Inc., which is dedicated to efficiency in local government in Columbus. He is a Mason and a Shriner. In addition, he serves as a trustee of Buckeye Boys' Ranch. In 1979 his company sponsored the National Revenue Tennis Classic, a Grand Prix tournament, all proceeds of which were contributed to the Ranch. He is an active supporter of the Columbus Association for the Performing Arts. His hobbies include being an avid pilot, and he maintains a corporate jet for executive travel.

Richard was born in Ypsilanti, Michigan, on August 2, 1950. He attended Eastern Michigan University in a pre-law program. He and his wife, Marva, live in Columbus.

RICHARD D. SCHULTZ

On August 6, 1978, an article appeared in the business section of the *Columbus Dispatch* about a budding new company, National Revenue Corporation. According to the *Dispatch*, the firm's net earnings would exceed $3 million for its twelve-month fiscal year and were projected to be $5 million for the following year—very impressive for a company founded only five years previously with an initial investment of $5,000! Just four days before the article's appearance Richard D. Schultz celebrated his twenty-eighth birthday. He is one of the most successful self-made entrepreneurs under thirty in the United States.

Richard originally wanted to practice law. While working during the summer as a law clerk, intending to go to law school that fall, he was offered a collection-agency job. "By the fifth week," he relates, "I had earned more commissions than the attorney I was clerking for. He had been out of law school for six years, and, at age twenty-one, I was able to earn more than he did. That was back in 1971, and that's when I decided to work full time as a salesman for Credit Control Company."

He smiles confidently. "I thrived on the fact that I could

work on a straight commission basis; I figured the only thing that could possibly hold me back was my own abilities. I was quite willing to put in all the effort it would require to succeed." By that fall he was offered a state manager's position in either New Jersey or Ohio, and he chose Ohio. "But I had some definite concepts about how a collection service should function. I'd discovered that nobody was happy with their collection agency, and, most important, they weren't satisfied with the service the company I worked for was providing them." He admits, "My ideas were rather provocative at the time." Finally he made a presentation to the company president on a revolutionary new approach he had developed. "He looked at me like I was crazy! He rejected everything I said. But I knew that my new concepts would work, and that's when I decided to quit and test them out for myself." The company he had worked for eventually went out of business.

When Richard entered the business, consumerism was at an all-time peak. "In fact," he asserts, "from 1967 to 1972 more consumer-oriented legislation regulating this industry was passed in this country than there had been in the previous fifty years. Suddenly all governmental bodies, statewide and national, became interested in regulating agencies that were collecting delinquent accounts. The Fair Credit Reporting Act was passed, and the Federal Trade Commission got into the act with the Guides Against Deception in the Collection of Delinquent Accounts. Also states began passing new licensing laws. They began to limit the remedies available to credit grantors and third-party collectors in collecting delinquent receivables. In retrospect, it is obvious that the industry's abusers had brought on justifiable public resentment."

To Richard, credit is the life blood of the U.S. economy. He recognized that consumers needed protection; but he also reasoned that the new wave of legislation would result in a tightening of credit, slowing down the economy. If the cash flow of American business declined, then prices would eventually increase.

"I realized that the average collection agency was collecting only about 30 percent of the money they were after. With the typical charge of 33 to 50 percent, their customer was only going to net 15 to 20 percent of the amount due him."

Richard's enthusiasm for his concepts is contagious. "With the industry's recovery ratio being so pathetically low, I believed that their timing in pursuing delinquent accounts must be wrong. They turned over accounts when they were from six to twelve months old. Why did a credit manager wait so long to turn them over? Because he didn't want a conventional collector alienating his customers and he wanted to avoid paying those high percentage charges that ranged from 33 to 50 percent of the amount an agency collects. (That's more than most creditors' profit margins.) On the other hand, with the accounts being so old and recovery ratios so low, the agency wouldn't be able to make ends meet if it charged a lower percentage. A vicious cycle was created. While a creditor concentrated on collecting 120-day accounts, trying to avoid those high percentage charges and customer alienation, the thirty- and sixty-day accounts became older; soon they became 120-day accounts!"

Since recovery ratios would be higher with not-so-old accounts, Richard felt that he could charge a creditor a much lower figure if he could persuade the creditor to turn over delinquent accounts when they were sixty to ninety days old. "Also," Richard says, "he could justify turning them over to us, because of our lower collection fee and the fact that we specialize in preserving the creditor's good will. So I set up a schedule that wasn't based on a percentage of the amount collected, but instead on a fixed fee for the services National Revenue would provide. Our fee structure ranges from $6.25 to a maximum of $150." *Industry Week* magazine reported that NRC recently collected $48,000 for a customer and it cost him only $58. If he had turned the account over to an attorney, the law firm would have immediately charged him 33 percent.

Creditors now had a true incentive to turn over their delinquent accounts in sixty to ninety days, thereby reducing the creditor's internal costs. With National's help, clients began to witness recovery ratios two to three times higher than previous ones. Soon the clients could concentrate on thirty- to sixty-day accounts, which resulted in higher cash flows. In effect, National Revenue not only offered a means to collect past-due debts, but at the same time could considerably increase cash flow while preserving the creditor's community image.

Richard feels that National provides *preventive* maintenance. "We can't come into a customer and say, 'Give me your old garbage accounts, we're going to do a fabulous job collecting them for you.' Nobody can do that. We're in a highly regulated business and we use many of the same collection methods as our competition. But they seem to work only as salvage operations. We're an *alternative* to the tradition. You see, when I started, it was a matter of building a better mousetrap! I realized that a golden opportunity existed to *solve that problem.* I truly believe that the tougher the problem is to solve, the greater the rewards will be. When you really think about it, if there hadn't been any problems, how would National Revenue have come into being? If everybody could have solved the existing problems, then my company would have served no real purpose, and I wouldn't own and operate the largest firm in this industry today. It's really that simple, isn't it?

"In our system, our representative, an educated executive consultant, teaches a customer how to control write-offs from the beginning of credit-granting procedures to decisive court action when needed. We're offering a total-concept cash-flow management service. We not only show the client how to manage internal collection efforts, but we make it economically feasible for him to have us make his collections quickly for a fixed fee. We give him a complete A-to-Z service. If we don't make a collection, there's no charge. In this system, it's hard for us to have an unhappy customer!"

National Revenue employs more than 150 people at its new $3 million, ultra-modern corporate headquarters and computer center in Columbus. The installation of the computer with other systems and furnishings will be valued at another $2 million. The company presently has more than 600 representatives serving more than 40,000 firms throughout America. It currently holds about $100 million in assignments for collection. The firm is one of the nation's largest users of WATS telephone lines and Western Union mailgrams. Its accounts include everything from many of *Fortune's* top 500 corporations to thousands of "Mom and Pop" operations, and even a nudist colony.

How was he able to do it all so fast? Richard says with a chuckle, "It's like the question, 'How do you eat an elephant?' The answer obviously is: *One bite at a time.* It really boils down to establishing both short-term and long-term goals. I'm never satisfied, continually coming up with new ideas and more goals to strive for. People joke around here, 'Schultz's long-term planning is nine months.' But, in a sense, I feel that's a healthy attitude, because we're never satisfied where we are today. We're always looking ahead."

Richard points out that when he started in the business, he took advantage of an opportunity. However, today the licensing is considerably more difficult. "We have so many grandfather-type state licenses," he says. "Also, of the 5,000 collection agencies in the United States, about half belong to the American Collectors Association. The average member has eight employees; NRC is approximately 100 times bigger than the average agency. And with all of our sophisticated software and equipment and the top-grade management team we've put together, well, we just have a tremendous head start over any Johnny-come-latelies."

Like so many large companies, National Revenue Corporation had a humble beginning. After spending about a year working for other agencies, at age twenty-two, Richard founded his company. "I had about $5,000 to invest," he says, "so I obviously had to operate on a low overhead. I started the business in the spare bedroom of my apartment. I was the salesman; I made the first telephone calls; I even remember watching *Gunsmoke* while licking stamps and envelopes. I can look back and laugh now. I felt that I hit the big time when I bought a $6 stamp machine so I wouldn't have to lick stamps anymore! Today I have a $30,000 stamp machine, and we spend $15,000 to $20,000 each week just on postage.

"As the business grew, I hired a secretary who worked four hours a day. Later I employed full-time help. Sure, I had some interesting recruiting problems due to the fact that my office was in a bedroom, but I just had to work around it, that's all. It got to the point where my apartment was filled up with people and I had desks all over the place. As the business paid for itself, I hired more people and finally moved into an office building. I never had to borrow a dime."

Was his age a disadvantage? "Well, it was only when I *thought* it was. But I have always been a big believer in turning every disadvantage into an advantage. I discovered that when I interviewed a prospective salesman, I could easily convince him to come aboard after I took him out into the field so he could watch me *making money*. That was the greatest way to recruit. I would make $1,000 in commissions in a single day, and the guy would be jumping up and down! I would also call on banks that raved about our service, and I'd run into a satisfied customer who would be the most delighted person in the world. Soon my age was an advantage. Because I'd appear so average, the recruitee would think, 'Boy, if this guy could make so much money, I can do it too!' "

Richard's twenty-acre estate (including an indoor pool and sunken tennis courts) has a library containing just about every book ever written on salesmanship, motivation, and business management. He owns more than 500 tapes on these subjects. "I read every book on selling that I could get my hands on. I listened to every tape, and I attended every seminar. I wanted to be polished on all marketing concepts and sales strategies. When I met with people who had twenty to thirty years of selling experience, they really knew that I *knew* what I was talking about."

Richard doesn't hesitate to spend money to make more money. "I went first class in every way I could," he asserts. "I wanted the right image, and even my first offices were plush. I also believe in developing well-groomed, properly trained representatives. When I was out in the field with a potential customer, I wanted to create an image that could match anybody's. I feel that a good initial impression fosters confidence in the company. After all, in most cases, a customer's only personal contact with a company is with the salesperson. A firm's representative sets the stage for an eventual business relationship. I also made sure that we had the finest caliber of marketing tools. No company, including IBM, can walk into a prospect's office with any more sophisticated sales aids than we use. So, when my representative or I were out in the field, we were on even ground with anybody! And, most important, I *knew* that we could provide the very finest service ever available, and that kind of an attitude had to make a tremendous difference. Soon our salespeople and our customers knew it too!"

The representatives of National Revenue Corporation work on a straight commission basis, which Richard believes to be the most lucrative. "It's a fact that 80 percent of the people earning over $25,000 a year are doing it in a sales capacity based on incentive compensation," he claims. "In essence, commission selling is like a mini free-enterprise system. Each individual gets paid according to the effort put forth. The person who is most willing to pay dues will eventually come out on the top. Of course, that individual must be the most motivated, the most skilled—and, in addition, exercise the most sweat of the brow. In turn, he or she will be most amply rewarded."

Richard emphasizes that salaried salespeople receive less income because the company protects itself against the bad weeks *all* the sales force will have. In this system the most productive people will receive a reduced income, and the nonproductive will eventually be fired. But if an individual develops the ability to generate business, he or she will always be able to earn a fine living. Even during a recession or a depression the want ads in every newspaper will have companies begging for good salespeople.

"I don't understand why most people always want to put a ceiling on their earning capacities. Even with my company, we have one man who's been with us for three years, and he'll work on Monday and Tuesday and sometimes on Wednesday, but the rest of the time he's out on the golf course. Now he averages about $1,000 a week in commissions, but he sets a ceiling on himself, and when he reaches a certain income, he just plain stops working! It reminds me about the old story about how they train a flea in a flea circus. You know, they put a glass on top of him, and the flea keeps jumping up and hitting his head on the glass. Soon he stops trying, and when the glass is removed, the flea never jumps any higher than the level where the glass had been. Some employees set such limits. The more they think about such ceilings, the more they become what they think about themselves. Success at NRC is based on unlimited earning opportunity for ambitious people. One man, Tom Speiss of Philadelphia, for example, went from $30,000 a year to over $250,000 in just twenty-four months!

"I never put a ceiling on my people—or myself," Richard continues, "although I personally always set what I considered to be attainable goals. I first wanted to earn $100,000 a year, and when I reached that goal, I set another goal at $1 million. Now my goal is set at $5 million. In other words, I believe that you have to have interim stops. Naturally, I didn't set a $5 million goal at age twenty-two. But I've never put a ceiling on myself, and I never will."

The no-ceiling philosophy, plus the personal success so many people associated with the company have achieved, is symbolized by a gift presented to Richard by NRC managers throughout the country. It is a bronze bust of him done by the nationally acclaimed sculptor Joel Hurst, who has sculpted John Wayne and several United States Presidents.

There is no ceiling on the market for NRC's services either. In 1960 the total consumer indebtedness was $56 billion; by 1970 it had doubled to $112 billion. It rose to $185 billion by 1975 and increased to $225 billion by the end of 1977. "That's only consumer indebtedness," Richard adds. "Those figures don't include corporate accounts payable, which average closer to $700 billion, and the bulk of National Revenue's volume is commercial. It's presently running at 65 percent of our total sales, which are growing at almost 300 percent per year."

What's to prevent other companies from copying National Revenue's techniques? Richard grins. "Well, I have a stock answer for that one too. It goes like this: 'They copied all they could follow, but they couldn't copy my mind,/And I left 'em sweating and stealing, a year and a half behind.' That's a quote from Rudyard Kipling's nineteenth-century poem 'The "Mary Gloster."' It really sums up my attitude. With properly executed market penetration, and the broadening of our product base including such innovations as adding credit insurance, we'll always be a giant-sized step ahead of any competition. The company that we are today will not be able to compete with the company we're going to be a year from now."

WILLIAM G. McGOWAN

11

William G. McGowan

(MCI COMMUNICATIONS CORPORATION)

William G. McGowan is chairman of the board and chief executive officer of MCI Communications Corporation, a telecommunications company headquartered in Washington, D.C.

Bill founded the company in August, 1968, and as chief executive officer has guided MCI through regulatory applications, financing, system engineering and development, and construction. By 1978 MCI had annual revenues in excess of $87 million and a net income of nearly $5.2 million. In ten years the company, which competes with AT&T by offering long-distance telephone service to business and industry, has established a nationwide network of microwave stations.

Prior to founding MCI, Bill headed a New York City management and financial consulting firm which concentrated on high-technology industries. For the previous four years he headed the Ultrasonic Corporation, a company he founded in 1959. Ultrasonic was a pioneer in the development of cryogenic measurement devices for the U.S. space and missile programs. As an employee of the Magna Theatre Corporation he also participated in the development of the revolutionary Todd-AO process, the first application of seventy millimeter techniques to the motion-picture industry.

He began his association with Todd-AO in 1954, following his graduation from Harvard Business School with a Master's degree in business administration. At Harvard he was selected as a Baker Scholar. In 1952 Bill received his Bachelor of Science degree from King's College, Wilkes-Barre, Pennsylvania. He served with the U.S. Army as a noncommissioned officer in postwar Germany from 1946 to 1949.

Bill was born in Wilkes-Barre on December 10, 1927. He is a bachelor and lives in Washington, D.C.

When Bill McGowan founded MCI Communications in 1968, he believed that his company could provide better and more economical telecommunications service than was then being offered. At the time many people thought that only a madman would attempt such an enterprise. It meant meeting head-on the nation's largest corporation, AT&T, which enjoyed a monopoly on the country's telephone service. And establishing a nationwide network is a very expensive venture— a huge investment was required to enter the business. Furthermore, AT&T had been around for more than a century; its billions of dollars in assets exceeded the wealth of most nations.

Bill McGowan, however, is a highly motivated and determined individual. He believed that, because AT&T was so big and old, a fine opportunity existed to offer the American business community a new company with fresh ideas.

"In the aerospace industry," Bill explains, "I had been involved with communications in the missile program, and tremendous advances had been made in that area. I observed that the telephone industry had been ignoring the needs of the computer industry. The computer industry had grown quickly to an enormous size, and its people were accustomed to advanced technology being introduced on a routine basis. But with a hundred-year-old company like AT&T—well, frankly, it was extremely slow to introduce anything.

"The telephone company simply wasn't geared to meet the needs of commerce," the tall, well-groomed executive points out. "The telephone industry has had an absolute fetish about having one system, and if a customer had unique needs, it simply wasn't interested in satisfying them. The philosophy of the industry has traditionally been referred to as pots—'plain old telephone service'! Bell was just not willing to supply innovative services. The industry was primarily structured to sell to the homeowner. The business community was approached with the same marketing strategy, and it didn't make any sense, because people do things differently in business than they do as consumers. But Bell didn't care whether you wanted a black telephone put in your home or a complicated telecommunications system installed in your company. You were going to be treated the same. Even their invoices were identical. And the representatives who called on you were going to be the same people."

After pausing briefly to light a cigarette, he continues, "I believed that we could succeed if we specialized in telecommunications services for the business community. Businesses would understand and appreciate good merchandising, and they would welcome products directed to their special needs. The part of the industry which looked most attractive was long-distance service. Local telephone service is typically granted to one company because it's desirable to have only one company digging up the streets and interconnecting the local telephones. But there was no more need to have one company connect all the long-distance services together than there is to have only one airline handle all the commercial airline service in the United States.

"You must understand that the telephone industry evolved in this country to include twenty-three Bell companies. Each of them is a very good size. There are also 1,500 independent local companies. AT&T was the company that interconnected them all, the Bell companies and the independents. And this ability to interconnect them was what gave AT&T control over the entire industry. Sure, they had twenty-three local operating companies with franchises to provide telephone service, but these locals had never been given franchises to provide long-distance telephone service. So I believed there was a need to provide the customer with better service, and plenty of room for competition. This competition would not only provide better service, but, frankly, it would spur Bell to do a better job."

Bill had extensive experience operating his own management and financial consulting firm in New York City prior to his involvement with MCI. His consulting firm concentrated in high-technology industries. This was the area of his expertise; he had founded Ultrasonic Corporation, which pioneered in the development of cryogenic measurement devices for the U.S. missile and space programs. After raising $50,000 and "literally working out of a garage in Hicksville, Long Island" during the first year of Ultrasonic, he developed major contracts with large aerospace contractors. The company eventually went public, and later, after selling his interest, Bill became a consultant.

"I ended up with enough money not to have to worry about making a living," he says. "I was intrigued with new products and services, and I had become attracted to ideas which hadn't been put into effect before. Frankly, I enjoyed the challenge of doing things that didn't have a set pattern, so I was constantly looking for products which hadn't yet been introduced to the marketplace. As people became aware of my interests, they came to me with different opportunities. I helped these businesses with their funding and initial organization, and I was really enjoying myself.

"In 1968 a Chicago attorney told me about an interesting client of his in Joliet, Illinois, who was having financial troubles. There were four principals in a mobile-radio business which sold two-way radios, mainly to police, truckers, and taxi companies. They wanted to build a small microwave system between Chicago and St. Louis to service truckers on Route 66 and people on the canal barges.

"I investigated this company as I did a lot of others. Out of 1,000 ideas brought to me, I'd probably look at 100 and perhaps negotiate ten of those to end up with one. This mobile-radio company, Microwave Communications, Inc., was thinly capitalized by a man named John Goeken, along with his family and friends. They were having all kinds of problems trying to get their application filed with the Federal Communications Commission, because the telephone company was opposing them.

"Goeken had met with fierce resistance from Bell, and I felt that it would be necessary to establish a company in Washington with experts to deal with the FCC [Federal Communications Commission]," Bill adds. "I also believed that once we were looked upon as the company with expertise in engineering and the marketplace we could attempt to obtain regional common carriers to serve various sections of the country. I didn't think it made any sense to have only a small company in one isolated area of the country—there had to be a national system."

The New York–based management and financial consultant had the venture-capital background which would provide the necessary know-how for Goeken's private-line communications concept. Bill reasoned that his newly formed Washington headquarters would be the foundation of an eventual network of regional carriers throughout the country. A separate corporation was formed, and investors in various markets were contacted to invest in regional carriers. The Chicago–St. Louis carrier became one of seventeen such common carriers, each a separate corporation. Others were formed, including one in New England which covered Massachusetts, Vermont, and Connecticut and interconnected with a New

York–to–Washington company; and later a New York–to–Chicago system.

The financial package for each of these corporate entities was three-tiered. There was an initial investment of $500,000, sufficient to prepare and file the company's application and prosecute it through comparative hearing. The next step was a loan commitment from the investors, typically for $1.5 million, accompanied by options, callable only upon FCC award of construction permits. The investor loans were to see the company through its staffing and development stages into commercial operation. Finally, the construction and components of the system were to be financed, turnkey, by the equipment supplier, with equal payments commencing six months after commercial operation and continuing for five years.

At first Bill approached investors who were venture-capital oriented. Among the early investors were many large corporations, such as United Artists Theatre Circuit, Holiday Inns, FMR Development Corporation, National Liberty Life, Allen & Co., Baker, Fentress & Co., Hornblower Weeks, Meredith Publishing, and Bechtel Corporation.

"I felt that it was very important in the beginning," Bill stresses, "to attract investors who would be recognized by future investors as sophisticated professionals. I also believed that this kind of investor would give us tremendous credibility with the FCC."

In each of the carriers MCI took a minority equity interest, typically between 30 and 40 percent. Their interest gave them regional control as well as network manageability. The MCI Washington headquarters consisted of about fifty people. Engineers were hired to design microwave systems. The marketing people developed a marketing-research team and solicited testimony from users around the country to demonstrate the need for MCI's service. And the company hired people with expertise in dealing with the complicated procedures of filing FCC forms and applications. In addition to

MCI attorneys, there were five communications-law firms led by Haley, Bader & Potts. Four of the "Big Eight" accounting firms were selected individually by the carriers to break new ground in utility accounting.

Bill correctly surmised that no single carrier could afford the professional expertise required to bring its application to the high degree of starched sophistication required by the FCC. But collectively they could. MCI served as a consultant to each of its affiliates, assisting in application preparation, following up the application once it was filed, serving as a Washington-based trade association, and developing customer leads for the emerging industry. MCI worked on a contractual basis with its affiliates and collected fees for these services.

"These seventeen carriers were not able to offer any services until the FCC granted them a license," Bill explains, "and MCI was acting as their representative in Washington. They were paying us to get their applications approved. Until we did that, we couldn't consider constructing the systems. We had seventeen shells and our Washington office, which was one small operating unit being supported by the fees generated in servicing the shells."

While MCI was formed in 1968, it was not until June, 1971, shortly after Dean Burch's appointment as chairman of the FCC, that all applications were processed. "It was actually much faster than anyone ever expected," Bill confesses. "The FCC concluded that there was a need for our service, and that the public should be given a choice. It was reasoned that this would encourage innovation throughout the industry in long-distance service."

In this landmark ruling, which became known as "The MCI Decision," the FCC stated that all qualified applicants would be afforded "the freedom to fail." In addition to MCI, the FCC approved applications from four other companies to construct competing domestic satellite systems that would provide long-distance communications. The FCC was looking for demonstrated functional strength to serve the public interest. The Commission saw no adverse impact on AT&T from "full and fair competition" in private-line services. All the premises upon which MCI and its affiliates had been organized and financed were changed by the FCC decision. With open entry, there was no need for regional carriers. Setting up a national network was the obvious direction for MCI to take. It was agreed by all carriers that they would be merged into one company and obtain stock in MCI. So MCI emerged as a strong network operator, industry coordinator, advocate, and sales force.

To secure the level of funding necessary to support these new roles, MCI began an aggressive capital-raising program. Between May, 1971, and February, 1972, equity with and without options and warrants was offered. The company sold millions of shares of preferred stock at $2.50 per share in three private placements. In November, 1971, MCI authorized 2 million shares of preferred stock and sold 255,000 Series A preferred shares, together with an option to purchase 60,000 shares of common stock, the subsequent exercise of which increased proceeds from the entire transaction to $2.7 million. During the three months from December, 1971, through February, 1972, MCI sold 852,000 additional common shares for a total of $7.1 million, together with warrants to purchase at $9.17 per share another 242,914 common shares. Purchasers included the English Rothschilds via New Court Securities, Henry Ansbacher & Co., Ltd., the English merchant bank, and private United States investors. MCI was diligently scrutinized by each participant in these transactions, whose involvement with the company at this stage of development, though clearly still venturesome, was characterized as "mezzanine venture capital" participation. A public offering was completed in June, 1972, in an underwriting in which 26 percent of MCI, or 3.3 million shares, was sold at $10 per share. The net proceeds to the company exceeded $30 million.

"It was the largest venture-capital underwriting in the history of Wall Street," Bill notes with apparent satisfaction. "Our investment banker, Blyth, Eastman, Dillon (then Blyth & Co.), agreed for the first time in their history to bring public not only a company without an earnings history but also a developmental venture valued in excess of $100 million."

Together with a five-bank credit agreement and the private placements, the public offering meant that MCI had more than $120 million in available capital.

"With the necessary capital," the MCI chairman expounds, "we started a massive construction program, employing techniques that had only been used in isolated military cases. Instead of constructing buildings and repeaters around the country, we had prefabricated shelters designed, and put all of the equipment into them in a central location at Richardson, Texas. We shipped them out on lowboy carriers, and meanwhile we completed the construction of the towers, fences, and other equipment.

"Instead of spending months like the telephone company, which constructs microwave repeaters with its people living in hotels and motels at construction sites, we were able to get our construction time down to four hours for moving in the shelter, connecting it, and operating it. That's because we had already prefabbed it. And we did everything ourselves. The only thing we jobbed out was the civil part of it, like building a road, putting in a fence or a concrete pad or a building tower. We assembled and tested everything at our Texas location, so we knew it would work. We then shipped the units out to the sites and simply turned the system on. In early 1973 we were actually building at the rate of one microwave site per day."

Each microwave site has an antenna facing another approximately twenty-five to forty miles away, depending on the terrain. A radio signal with a frequency well above that of television is transmitted. Each antenna can carry twelve or more frequencies, each frequency capable of carrying as many as 2,100 voice channels from tower to tower.

MCI initially serviced the largest markets in the United States, but it developed long-range plans to cover every market throughout the country. "We were like any company who introduces a new product," Bill states. "You start off by marketing it in one area and you gradually expand. Television, for instance, was only available in New York City when it first came out."

The first service offered by MCI was called dedicated private lines, known today as leased lines. There are several types, including tie lines, foreign-exchange lines, and inter-machine trunks. Each leased line is assigned to a specific user, who pays a flat monthly rate based on distance, the number of leased lines, and total MCI circuit lines used. These leased lines are basically identical to Bell System private lines, the major difference being that MCI's rates are substantially lower than AT&T's.

"The primary reason we could save our customers money," Bill explains, "is that we could build a microwave system far less expensively than Bell. They have been operating over the years as a rate-base company, and they developed practices and patterns which resulted in enormously expensive plants and equipment. As somebody once said, 'The phone company has given us a Cadillac of telephone service, but at a Rolls Royce price.' The phone company tends to over-invest in everything it does. For example, we'll go out and lease a plot of land from a farmer and place a small tower on it without interfering with the farming. But the telephone company will purchase acres of land and construct a magnificent building. You'd be happy to *live* in some of these beautiful concrete-and-steel edifices.

"We're also able to operate far less expensively," Bill stresses. "We can do the same job as AT&T with one third the personnel! Their organization is more than 100 years old, and their multilayered structure has become extremely inefficient.

"It's important to note, too, that they're a guaranteed-profit company, so they've never had any real incentive to be competitive. There's never been pressure to become efficient. For instance, if they go out and spend $100 million in institutional advertising, with their ego ads telling the public 'how good the system is,' it doesn't actually cost them anything because they can build all those advertising expenses into their rates and *then* get a percentage of those expenses added in on top—really pure profit! Sure, the regulators are supposed to look at their expenses, but there's no way an actual restraint is placed on Bell, and they pass all expenses on to the customer with rate increases.

"As a rate-base company, their profits are also regulated. Having a monopoly position, they have to accept that limitation. But they're also guaranteed a profit! So what's happened over the years is that, without a spur of competition, they've just been free to build and build, without having to be efficient like a profit-motivated company. Consequently, they've enjoyed a very good life. But we're using the latest equipment, and we're operating at about one third their cost. So we can provide the services for far less expense and at a far lower price. *And we can still make a very good profit.*"

After the 1971 FCC ruling granting competitors the right to engage in long-distance communications, AT&T challenged certain aspects of the new policy and would not allow MCI the same interconnection facilities that it received from the local telephone companies. AT&T became concerned about losing its monopolistic position when it discovered that MCI had captured over 80 percent of the point-to-point private-line service between Chicago and St. Louis just twenty months after opening its services between the two cities. Bell complained that specialized common carriers like MCI concentrated on high-traffic, low-cost routes, and were thus able to establish lower rates in those markets—they called this "cream skimming."

A spokesman for AT&T stated, "We realize that coming

out against competition is like coming out against apple pie, but if we don't come out and fight what affects your phone bill, who will?" AT&T further maintained that it is a "natural monopoly" that can serve the public most efficiently and at the lowest cost when it has "complete end-to-end responsibility for service." It reasoned that competition would lead to reduced efficiency and higher phone bills.

"Apparently AT&T had decided that the best competitive weapon is to prevent competition," Bill counters. He claims that Bell had "reactionary" policies reflecting the "rigidity and intransigence of an established monopoly."

A concerned look appears on his face. "Bell refused to allow us to connect our microwave system to our customers' offices through the local telephone company's circuits. So, even though we had sold our service to a customer, AT&T had instructed the local phone companies not to provide us with their service for our customers—although we were willing to pay like anyone else. They had decided to kill competition. AT&T didn't like what the government had decided, so they were going to ignore the law. We had all of our systems, towers, buildings, and people, but we couldn't deliver. It was somewhat like a long-distance airline, which is an accurate description of us because we are also in the transfer business. We transfer information rather than people. However, the competition owned all the airports and wouldn't allow us to land.

"It was a total disaster." Bill shakes his head. "We couldn't get any revenue, and our expenses kept going on. It was like running an airline—whether you have ten or 150 customers, there's very little difference in cost. We had the system up, but we couldn't provide the service.

"By September, 1973, it had really come to a crisis. AT&T stated that they thought the government was wrong, and they would not provide us their interconnecting service. By that time we had spent $80 million or so, and we were in a state approaching panic. We went to anybody who would listen to us. The FCC agreed with our complaint and sent AT&T a letter, but it was ignored. We went to the Justice Department, and they also thought we were reasonable and started investigative proceedings. They issued a CID [Civil Investigation Directive] which allowed them to get papers and documents from the phone company. We brought an antitrust suit against AT&T; however, we recognized that it could take years, when what we needed was immediate action. Finally, on December 29, 1973, several months after this whole disaster began, a federal court in Philadelphia issued a mandamus directing AT&T to order their people to give us the connections with our customers.

"It had been a crucial period for us." He sighs. "We had many people on our payroll with nothing to do, and we had to reduce our work force drastically. Because we needed working capital to keep the ship afloat, we had to get additional funds from our creditors. And you can imagine how intimidated our customers were—the largest corporation in the world had announced that it didn't want us around. We were facing the worst possible circumstances, because we hadn't finished enough of the system to be viable. So, even if Bell gave us everything we wanted, which they weren't about to do anyway, we were committed to plant and equipment expansion.

"Even today I don't think we have the cooperation from the local telephone company that we should have. We *should* get the same service as any other customer when we want to interconnect our long lines with an AT&T customer, but the local telephone company looks on us as a competitor. I don't think it's the local phone people themselves, because I believe that they're trying to do a professional job. I feel that it's typically at the policy-making level, and the local Bell companies are handicapped because they've been given orders by AT&T and have little choice in the matter. But slowly and painfully we've been getting our rights, forcing them through any method we could, sometimes embarrassing the telephone company publicly in front of the FCC. At other times, when they couldn't give us a reason why they wouldn't service us, it's been outright confrontation. And there have been instances when the FCC had to force them to serve us. We've learned how to work around their slow-rolling techniques, but unfortunately we have had cases where our customers simply lost heart. On the other hand, a great number of our customers wanted AT&T to have competition and did not appreciate the fact that the phone company wanted to do away with an alternative supplier.

"Over a period of time, we realized that AT&T was never going to be fully cooperative," Bill continues, "at least not in the time frame in which we could become profitable. It therefore became evident that we had to start introducing other services which didn't require interconnecting with Bell equipment, so that we could avoid the hassle of dealing with the phone company. That's actually what prompted us to introduce Execunet in 1974."

Execunet is a long-distance metered service that offers a highly competitive rate to a customer, typically 25 to 35 percent less than AT&T's daytime rates. The user is given an access number which he dials to get connected with MCI's local Execunet equipment. The long-distance call is then transmitted by microwave towers. A sophisticated computer program measures each call according to time and area, and the customer is billed on a monthly basis. Presently the network covers most major markets throughout the United States. MCI plans to offer the service across the country, and new areas are continually being added to the system.

For the medium to large long-distance users, MCI developed its Network Service, in which a customer is tied in by a permanent connection to one of MCI's computer-controlled switches. The switch routes the customer's call so efficiently and economically to its distant MCI city destination that

Network Service users can, depending upon their calling volume, save as much as 75 percent of normal long-distance telephone charges.

MCI also offers computer-controlled long-distance calling at a fixed monthly charge plus usage. This service, which is available through MCI's own computers or those belonging to its customers, is called Telemanagement because it monitors how long-distance telephone calls should be made. The MCI computer will automatically decide the most economical way to place a call—whether it should be placed on a Bell line or an MCI line. The computer also gives outgoing calls priority according to the person placing the call. For example, the sales manager might have top priority if all company lines are temporarily tied up. At the end of each month, a report is submitted to the customer reviewing the exact usage of the company's telephone calls. Phone calls are broken down according to cost by every office division, and MCI makes recommendations for more effective application.

As an example of how creatively MCI customers can use the capacity that they lease from the company, take the automotive industry. An automobile buyer can specify precise model features for a new car, and if the car is not available at his dealer, the MCI system's facilities let the auto maker's computers come on line to poll all the existing automobiles at different dealers throughout the network. The inventory search occurs during the evening nonworking hours. If a requested automobile is not available, it will be assembled the following day. This service permits automobile dealers to supply truly customized cars and still keep inventories to a minimum, thus realizing significant savings. A similar service enables retailers across the nation to be in constant contact with their branch stores, suppliers, regional warehouses, shippers, and everyone else essential to the orderly flow of the goods they require. Another MCI service connects a traveler who dials an airline's local telephone number with the airline's reservations operations in a distant city.

The effect of these MCI features is quicker service to the consumer as well as significant savings. "It used to be that when an individual went into business, he'd be local," Bill says. "But today business people look at the entire country and even the world as their marketplace."

Bill takes a short puff on his cigarette and enthusiastically adds, "We have all sorts of new products on the drawing boards. One of these days we'll offer electronic mail. So far it's been the cost that has kept the facsimile industry from being a reality. But I see no reason why we shouldn't some-day be able to transmit correspondence nearly immediately, or at the very least have it sitting on somebody's desk any-where in the country by the next morning. And once a com-pany's equipment is programmed, it could be used at night very inexpensively.

"Now, I'm not talking about just computer information with digital print-outs," Bill continues. "I'm referring to elec-tronic mail, sending written documents by telecommunica-tions. Can you imagine a letter instantly appearing on a screen at the receiver's terminal? And then when he pushes a button, a hard copy prints out right in front of him!"

MCI Communications Corporation is an excellent example of America's free-enterprise system being able to operate in a fully competitive environment. The consumer is the ultimate beneficiary of this daring company's innovation and econo-mies. MCI also illustrates how a highly motivated group of business people in a small company can compete head-on with a giant corporation like AT&T.

"We've just been a classic example of how a small com-pany can be quick on its feet and responsive to change," Bill concludes. "AT&T, on the other hand, illustrates how a giant corporation tries to protect itself with committees—and their analyzing and forecasting may take four years before they're ready to take action. A company must be able to act quickly and confidently, because today will be different from tomor-row."

Finally, Bill McGowan is an entrepreneur who recognized a need in an industry monopolized up to that time by America's largest corporation, and who refused to be denied the right to compete.

12

John Z. De Lorean

(DE LOREAN MOTOR COMPANY)

John Z. De Lorean is the chairman of the board and president of De Lorean Motor Company, a publicly held corporation headquartered in New York City.

John began his career in the automobile industry in 1952 as an engineer with Packard Motor Car Corporation. By 1956, at age thirty-one, he headed the Packard research and development program. Later that year, knowing that Packard was phasing out of the automotive industry, John joined General Motors Corporation as director of advanced engineering of the Pontiac Division. He served as assistant chief engineer of the Pontiac Division from 1959 to 1961, and as chief engineer from 1961 to 1965. In 1965, at age forty, he became the youngest man ever to head a division at General Motors when he was made general manager of the Pontiac Division.

In 1969 John was promoted to the post of general manager of the Chevrolet Motor Division, again the youngest man ever to hold that position. In 1972 he became group vice-president in charge of all North American car and truck operations. Under his leadership 1973 production exceeded 7 million vehicles with a retail value approaching $40 billion. The operation generated 87 percent of General Motors' total profits.

By then John was acknowledged both inside and outside the corporation as a leading candidate for its presidency; yet in 1973, at age forty-eight, he startled the business world by resigning his position.

Upon leaving General Motors, John served one year as the president of the National Alliance of Businessmen, an organization devoted to finding jobs for disadvantaged Americans. In 1974 he formed the John Z. De Lorean Corporation, a consulting firm whose clients included such companies as W. R. Grace, Ryder Systems, Chris Craft Industries, Piper Aircraft, and Sears, Roebuck & Company, as well as several foreign governments. In addition to providing consulting services, the firm also helped clients acquire sales and licensing rights for products and engineering techniques. Most important, it was the nucleus of the De Lorean Motor Company, which John formed in October, 1975.

John presently has a part ownership in the New York Yankees, and he formerly held an interest in the San Diego Chargers. He owns two ranches in Idaho and an avocado farm in California.

He received a Bachelor of Science degree in mechanical engineering from the Lawrence Institute of Technology, and a Master's degree in automotive engineering from the Chrysler Institute in 1952. Later he earned a Master's degree in business administration at the University of Michigan. Forty-four U.S. patents have been awarded to him, many for engine innovations, others for advances in the design of transmissions, suspensions, brakes, and body details.

John was born in Detroit on January 6, 1925. He is married to Cristina Ferrare, a top fashion model and actress. They have two children, Zachary Tavio and Kathryn Ann, and live in New York City.

Since the first flivvers coughed and bucked their way down dusty lanes, Americans have talked about making automobiles better. John Zachary De Lorean is actually doing something about it.

De Lorean's whole life has been intertwined with automobiles. He was a child of Detroit, which has given the world at least as many dreams as Hollywood and punched them out of the cold, hard reality of steel rather than of ephemeral images. His father worked at the very heart of the auto business, in a Ford foundry. John De Lorean soon became part of its brains.

His ability, his imagination, his zest for the business drove him at turbo-charged speeds to the top of that very competitive business. He was only forty when he became general manager of Pontiac in 1965, the youngest person ever to head a General Motors division. Four years later GM entrusted him with its bread and butter, the Chevrolet Division. Again he was the youngest ever. He was forty-seven when he became group vice-president in charge of North American car and truck operations in 1972, with responsibility for the sale of more than 7 million vehicles a year, at a retail value of nearly $40 billion. It was not a position given lightly; it accounted for 87 percent of GM's total profits.

It was all there for him: wealth, power, fame. The presidency of GM, the world's largest corporation, beckoned. All John had to do was want it. He didn't. He astonished the business world in 1973 by resigning from GM.

As one automotive executive put it, "De Lorean is the only man to fire General Motors." While some outside the industry shouted their approval and a few inside whispered theirs, most Americans viewed De Lorean's action with amazement. Was he a modern hero, or was he a kamikaze? They knew the Biblical question: "For what benefit will it be to a man if he gains the whole world but forfeits his soul?" The whole world was one thing. But General Motors? Many people would do anything for the opportunity that John rejected.

The dynamic entrepreneur calmly explains, "I didn't feel like I was in the game anymore. I was being promoted from division manager, which is like playing the quarterback, to a group executive, which is like being the owner of the stadium. I just didn't care much for staff activity, and the thought of doing it for the next seventeen years was oppressive."

John's eyes shine as he adds, "I suppose it's always been my dream to build my own automobile company. The DMC-12 represents certain qualities which I want to exist in a car. It will have unique ethical characteristics. It is designed to be fuel-efficient, and conservative of human life and resources. Since it will be made of totally noncorrosive materials, it will last for many, many years. I suppose I hoped someday to exhibit the ultimate of my art as an engineer."

John admits having his own thoughts on how to build cars. But he hopes to serve as an inspiration to others. "What has made this country was the people who believed in something and went out and did it," he declares. "But the magnitude of business today makes that tough. I'd like to demonstrate that a bunch of little guys with a dream can still do it."

Although John isn't a "little guy" in the ordinary sense of

JOHN Z. De LOREAN

the term, having already made it once in a big way in the automobile industry, he quickly admits that De Lorean Motor Company is "a gnat compared to GM." The first year's production of the DMC-12 was projected at 10,000 units, increasing to 25,000 the next year. John's long-range goal is 30,000 cars a year. Those are pretty low figures compared to the 7 million cars and trucks his divisions produced at GM back in 1973.

Starting an automobile company represents a very bold venture. The last American to succeed was Walter P. Chrysler, back in 1925. The graveyard of auto makers who have failed is studded with such names as Hudson, Studebaker, Packard, Kaiser, Willys, Tucker, and scores of lesser-known entrepreneurs who couldn't survive the competition of Detroit's Big Three. The huge start-up costs make it even more formidable today than in the past.

John refutes the idea that these failures mean his attempt will not succeed. "You had a lot of people who were not experienced in the auto business," he points out. "Study the postwar failures: Henry J. Kaiser was a shipbuilder, Preston Tucker worked in the Briggs factory, and Mal Bricklin's primary business experience was in hardware down in Florida. I never worked anywhere in my life except in the automobile industry."

John looks thoughtful. "I think perhaps the best advice you can give an individual who's about to start a new business," he emphasizes, "is to tell him to do it in a business that he knows. Some people may make money in businesses they don't know, but I think that's almost accidental."

John doesn't deny that his enterprise is a difficult one. "Even my closest friends are divided," he confesses. "Half of them think that this is approximately the equivalent of building the Alaskan pipeline single-handed, and the other half think my prospects are very good. Of course, while the failures in the American automobile industry are highly visible, there have been many postwar successes in foreign countries, such as Porsche, Bavarian Motor Works, Ferrari, Honda, and Lotus. My dream and objective is for us to someday in a small way emulate the success of BMW—they are an incredible company."

An examination of his track record at GM indicates that if anyone today can successfully start an automobile company, John is certainly that man. During his rapid rise at GM—a modern-day phenomenon—he demonstrated a rare combination of technical and marketing skills. As assistant chief engineer and chief engineer of the Pontiac Division, he was responsible for a succession of innovations that made Pontiac the talk of the entire industry. His contribution to the wide-track chassis design gave Pontiac a competitive edge it held for many years. John also noted that the X-type chassis frames then in use provided inadequate protection in side impacts, and he initiated Pontiac's changeover to the perimeter-type frame, which has its main sidemember at the outer sills. This design, which has since been adopted by every American auto that uses a separate frame, offers the advantages of lower cost, smoother running and more passenger room.

John also helped develop the 1961 Tempest, the first front-engined American-made car to have a rear-mounted transaxle and all-independent suspension. With a solid member linking the engine and transaxle together, the Tempest pioneered techniques that are now being rediscovered by European auto-makers.

While heading Pontiac's engineering, John contributed many design techniques, such as the articulated wiper blade for better windshield coverage, and the wiper that's concealed when not in operation. Another is the radio antenna built into the windshield glass. He also introduced the spring resistance to allow lane-change signaling that's now part of all directional signals. John expanded the use of plastics. Innovations under his direction included the first body-colored plastic-surface bumpers, and the first front end made of sheet molding compound with the first plastic grills and fender extensions.

He introduced the cogged rubber belt to drive an overhead camshaft, now a standard item in the auto industry worldwide. Many of the forty-four U.S. patents he has been awarded are for engine innovations. Others represent advances in the design of transmissions, suspensions, brakes, and body details.

While John was general manager of Pontiac, his emphasis on quality led to the establishment of a special facility to check the condition of finished cars and rectify any errors before the cars were shipped to dealers. By John's last full year at Pontiac, sales had almost quadrupled, from 229,831 units in 1958 to 877,302 units in 1968, and the division's market share had risen from 4.94 percent to a phenomenal 9.33 percent. Under his leadership Pontiac became the third-best-selling car in the nation. The 1969 Grand Prix, designed under his guidance, was based on GM's intermediate chassis instead of its full-size models. Soon the entire industry followed with intermediate-based personal luxury cars, such as the popular Chevrolet Monte Carlo and the Oldsmobile Cutlass. These "A Specials" were GM's largest-selling body styles until their redesigning for the 1978 model year.

In 1969 John was promoted to the position of general manager of Chevrolet. This division, although the world's leading vehicle producer, had suffered seven consecutive years of declining profits. By 1971, under his guidance, Chevrolet had become the first nameplate in the world to sell more than 3 million cars and trucks in a single year. Two years later Chevrolet took over the lead held by Ford in truck sales. With the tremendous sales at Chevrolet, the division's profits rose dramatically, but not at the expense of the dealers. Chevrolet dealers realized an increase in profits of more than 300 percent!

In his capacity as group vice-president in charge of all

GM's North American car and truck operations, a position he assumed in 1972, John became involved in the corporation's policy groups for marketing, engineering, research, industrial and public relations, and personnel administration and development. In these groups he crusaded for the practice of ethical business conduct, in-depth research on advanced power units, programs to benefit the disadvantaged, and cars which would not only meet but exceed safety and emission standards mandated by the government.

Following his resignation from GM, he spent about a year as president of the National Alliance of Businessmen, an organization devoted to finding jobs for disadvantaged Americans. Then, in 1974, he formed a consulting firm, the John Z. De Lorean Corporation, and took on as clients not only American businesses but several foreign governments as well. As a consultant, John put his reputation on the line by agreeing to participate in any losses as well as the profits resulting from his firm's recommendations. In this venture, his first exposure as an entrepreneur, he realized an annual income in excess of $2 million. It was during this period that he formulated his plans to fulfill his longtime dream, and in October, 1975, the De Lorean Motor Company became a reality.

John confesses that the transition from GM executive to entrepreneur was not an easy one. While his experience in the automobile industry gave him the necessary know-how to arrange for the design, engineering, and construction of a car, he knew nothing about raising the millions of dollars required to finance his new business venture. "As an operating executive at GM," he explains, wincing, "all I knew about financing was that if you needed $500 million to build a foundry somewhere, you'd fill out a form and send it off and a few months later a big thing would come back with all these signatures saying, 'Go ahead and spend the $500 million.' GM had an infinite amount of wealth. But that's not the way it works when you're one lone engineer trying to finance a car!

"With the combination of jobs I had in the automobile industry," he continues, "I didn't know anybody in the investment banking community or, for that matter, in any other industry. I knew absolutely nothing about raising money. Since the go-go days of the sixties when it only took an idea to have money thrown at you, the venture-capital market had simply become nonexistent. So we had to be very creative. We literally had to *invent* our own formula for raising money, and I think it turned out to be very good."

An estimated $200 million was raised to finance the De Lorean Motor Company. Through a series of complex fundraising efforts and from such varied sources as new-car dealers and Wall Street investment houses, about $40 million has been raised in the United States. Private investors include TV star Johnny Carson, who has invested $500,000 (part of that deal includes first rights to be the public spokesman in sales promotions for the car). Another $25 million comes from the French auto maker Renault, and the balance, about $140 million, comes from the British government in various forms, to be repaid over a period of years.

John believes that one of his biggest manpower problems stems from the fact that the American automobile industry has no other small companies. "It's only possible to hire experienced people from the big companies," he points out, "and, unfortunately, these people don't have the broad capability we need to operate a small company. It's necessary for our people to be able to do everything. When I was at GM, there were many things that I had my staff people do which I now must do for myself. If I need a cash-flow analysis, I do it. If I need a forecast, or have a report to write, nine times out of ten I'm the guy who does it. But despite this problem in finding people, we're building an incredible organization, and, size for size, we've got the best bunch of people of any company in the business today.

"The automobile business is also different from other businesses," he emphasizes. "We can't start this business in a small way. It's not like a company manufacturing a new soap. They can make a sample lot of bars and take them to some small town in the Midwest to try them out. We can't do that here, because by the time we've manufactured enough cars to do a test market, we've already spent all the money. So we must either come out with our product all the way or not even bother. *We have to be right!"*

Just how does an individual go about starting an automobile company? The first step John took was to form a small organization of a few engineers and some marketing people. "I had my concepts," he explains, "but I had to confirm that my dreams did in fact make good sense. Once we established a market, we did a little preliminary design work on it, and then we started to design and develop a car. After that, we built our prototypes."

Operating with a small group of hand-chosen key executives, the small automobile company began to grow. Today the De Lorean Motor Company has its corporate headquarters in New York City with its marketing and domestic development offices in Los Angeles. The research and development are based in Detroit. The company's designing is being done in Italy, and engineering is developed with the help of Lotus Cars, Ltd., in Norwich, England.

Finding a manufacturing site was a major undertaking for the neophyte car-maker. The company began investigating sites in 1975, and John considered many locations, meeting with officials in Texas, Pennsylvania, Alabama, Detroit, Wales, Spain, Ireland, and Puerto Rico. For a while it looked as if the assembly facility would be in Puerto Rico, and in April, 1977, a tentative commitment was made with the government of Puerto Rico. The company stopped seeing other suitors for about four months, until several problems arose. There were questions concerning the title of the site, and when the company's principal government contact resigned, De Lorean Motor Company began to investigate other locations. Finally, on the tip that General Motors was about to announce a seatbelt factory near Belfast in Northern Ireland,

John met with the British government and, as he says, "In an incredible forty-five days the deal was done." The company's production will take place at a 750,000-square-foot assembly facility located on a seventy-two acre site at Dunmurry, six miles west of central Belfast.

Although John will have invested an estimated $4 million of his own funds, he feels the most important thing "on the line" is his own reputation. "When a guy's spent his entire life successfully working in industry, his reputation is the most valuable thing he has," the immaculately groomed executive explains.

"A man doesn't do what I'm doing for the money," John claims. "If I were motivated by money, I'd be a deal maker. The first couple of years after I got out of General Motors, I made almost $3 million a year doing other things, which were really quite easy. I did some consulting; I put some deals together. But starting a company like this is something you don't do for money. First of all, I put a lot of my own money into the business, and I expect to operate without an income of any consequence for a period of four to five years. I estimate that I will give up several million dollars in lost earnings during this period. Then, before I can sell any of my own stock, securities regulations say that we must have two consecutive years of earnings at a certain level. With our depreciation, that's going to be another five years or so. This means that I won't have had any substantial income for about ten years. By that time I'll be around sixty years old, and I'd certainly be better off with a few million dollars ten years younger than perhaps $15 million when I'm sixty. So money can't be the motivator."

As John describes his product, one can sense his sincerity and dedication to building a superior automobile. The DMC-12 is a gull-wing, two-passenger sports car styled by Giugiaro of Ital Design, Turin, Italy, the designer of the Maserati Bora, Maserati Merak, Alfa Romeo Alfetta GT, and other sports cars. Its gull-wing doors open upward. The six-cylinder engine is capable of propelling the 2,300-pound car from a standing start up to, and far beyond, the 55-mile-an-hour speed limit in half the time of most Detroit cars—0 to 60-mile-per-hour performance in about seven and one-half seconds, comparable to the Porsche 911.

The car is low-slung, wide, and angular with a ninety-four-inch wheel base, and roomy enough so John, who is six-foot-four, is comfortable behind the wheel. A 163-cubic-inch, 130-horsepower V-6 engine that is currently being used by Peugeot, Renault, and Volvo is mounted behind the rear wheels. The car has independent suspension and four-wheel disk brakes, and will be available with either automatic or manual transmission. Because of its light weight, power brakes and power steering will not be necessary.

Equipped with passive restraints, the DMC-12 is designed for driver and passenger survivability in an eighty-mile-per-hour-plus head-on collision. It gets twenty-three miles per gallon of gas in the city and thirty-two miles per gallon on the highway. The car is made of stainless steel and structural laminates so that it will not corrode. The exterior panels are man-made material covered with stainless steel to prevent rusting and increase strength. "In theory," John explains, "you could drive it for twenty to twenty-five years and nothing should happen to it. It's not designed for early obsolescence."

A broad smile flashes on his face as he paraphrases Henry Ford: "You can have any color you want as long as it's stainless."

The DMC-12 will be priced somewhere between the Corvette and the Porsche. According to information compiled by *Automotive News,* no single model of any sports car with a base list price in the range of $12,000 or more has had U.S. sales in excess of 20,000 units. Only three manufacturers (Datsun, BMW, and General Motors) have had sales of sports-car models approximating 20,000 units or more in the base price range of $8,000 or more. This information indicates that the DMC-12 must not depend on attracting potential purchasers solely from the ranks of existing sports-car owners to meet its anticipated production and sales goals of 30,000 units each year. In addition to the sports-car buyer, it will have to attract former buyers of luxury cars.

For the time being, it appears that meeting production and sales goals will not be a problem for De Lorean Motor Company. By April, 1979, almost a full year prior to the scheduled production of the DMC-12, the company had approximately 40,000 advance orders. "These orders are backed up by the dealers," John says confidently. "Each order is based on the individual dealer giving us a purchase commitment. For instance, one dealer in Houston called me the other day to report twenty-eight cars sold with a $2,500 nonrefundable deposit. These are buyers who aren't even sure what the exact price of the car is going to be! And that's typical."

The large number of advance orders can be traced to the company's ingenious distribution program. A network of dealerships is being established, which John expects will eventually include 400 experienced dealers. These dealers must purchase a minimum subscription for 2,500 shares of common stock at an aggregate purchase price of $25,000. Under the terms of his sales agreement with the company, the dealer must purchase a minimum of 50 to 150 cars within twenty-four-months following the initial production of the DMC-12. The dealer must also stock a specified inventory according to the number of cars he's committed to purchase. The exact size of the dealer's inventory is determined by the company, following a consultation with the dealer and taking into account projections of the potential sales volume of the local market. The dealers will be located throughout the United States to distribute the DMC-12 most effectively. Some of the dealers have two or more locations, so the actual number of DMC-12 outlets will undoubtedly exceed 400 locations.

The participation by the dealers in the ownership of De

Lorean Motor Company represents John's vision of how an automobile business should be run. "As I see it," he stresses, "the ideal motor company is one that is owned by the people who work there. Of course, I'm referring to everybody—including dealers. If a company could have everybody working for the same objective, it would be a model situation. And that's what we're trying to do at De Lorean Motor Company.

"When a dealer owns a piece of the company, he has a vested interest in our success. Of course, with a little luck the dealer's $25,000 investment may turn out to be worth as much as a quarter to a half million dollars. And if that happens, well, he's going to feel pretty good about the company."

Evidently John Z. De Lorean also feels pretty good about the company. While there are some detractors who aren't willing to accept the idea that a new automobile manufacturer can succeed in the United States, the company's founder and chief executive officer claims to be 95 percent certain it will be a winner.

John has the financing he thinks he needs, and he believes he has the market for his product. Now it is up to him to put the car of his dreams on the road.

Conclusion

EN·TRE·PRE·NEUR (an'trə·prə·ner'), *n.* person
who organizes and manages a business or industrial enterprise, taking the risk or loss and
getting the profit when there is one. [F, *entre-
prendre* undertake. See ENTERPRISE]

Perhaps now that you have read *The Entrepreneurs* you'll
feel as I do about Mr. Webster's rather drab definition of the
word *entrepreneur.* Without such descriptive terms as *innovative, highly motivated, tenacious, totally committed, enthusiastic,* and *dedicated,* I don't think that the word *entrepreneur* is adequately defined. Certainly the reader would not
really understand what entrepreneuring is all about.

The twelve stories you have just read represent real live
people who are currently engaged in managing thriving enterprises. Their stories show how the business world actually
operates. These are not dry theories but down-to-earth facts
of organizing, developing, and managing businesses. Each of
these individuals began with a dream and turned it into a reality. And just as these twelve entrepreneurs put a great
amount of hard work into building these businesses, so today
they continue to meet new challenges with vitality and imagination.

In fact, each entrepreneur stressed that no business can afford to stop growing. "You either go forward or backward;
you never stand still." Each of them emphasized that without
growth an organization cannot motivate its people and will

have difficulty retaining them. Similarly, a static company will lose its ability to attract new people.

The interviews show that these twelve entrepreneurs shared many ideas. They also had certain characteristics in common. A summary of these characteristics is not a cut-and-dried formula for success, but it may offer a clearer understanding about what it takes to be an entrepreneur.

The first requirement for any individual about to embark on a new business venture is a strong conviction about his concepts. In all probability, most of his well-meaning friends and relatives will try to discourage him. Mary Kay Ash invested her life's savings in Mary Kay Cosmetics when she and her husband founded the company in 1963. A month later he died, and she was advised by her attorney to liquidate the business immediately and recoup whatever cash there was or *she would be left without a cent!* Her accountant advised her that the company's commission structure made success impossible, and he too recommended that she quickly dispose of the new business. Rather strong warnings for a newly widowed woman to receive. Had she listened to their advice, one of America's leading cosmetics firms would never have been more than a dream.

Another widow, in her early twenties, was given practically identical advice when she was about to open her first service station. "Everyone advised me not to go into business," Mary Hudson recalls. "Of course, this was back in 1934, and we were right in the middle of the Depression, with unemployment around 12 percent. In those days women weren't supposed to work." A local business man told her, "Look, little girl, during the past year this station was opened and closed twice. Now, if those smart men could not be successful, I'm sure you're going to fail. And you don't look like you can afford to lose your money at this point in life." Such strong warnings would discourage many people in similar circumstances.

Gary Goranson received similar advice when he started

Tidy Car. "My friends, relatives, and everybody else kept telling me that I was nuts to take a gamble and go into business for myself," Gary recalls. "They advised me to get a $20,000-a-year job and be satisfied." He too persisted, because of his conviction that his idea would work.

Bill McGowan was advised against the telecommunications field in the face of AT&T's monopoly. Nevertheless, he was prepared to enter this highly capital-intensive business and to meet the telephone company head-on in expensive and time-consuming legal battles.

John De Lorean is another entrepreneur with strong convictions. He resigned a top position at General Motors, where it was rumored that he would someday have the presidency, to form De Lorean Motor Company. He was well aware that the last American to found an automobile company and survive was Walter Chrysler in 1925. The attempts of such men as Henry Kaiser, Preston Tucker, and Malcom Bricklin had ended in defeat. And De Lorean's competitors would be some of the largest and most powerful companies in the world.

An entrepreneur's conviction is often such that he is willing to risk financial ruin if his new business venture fails. Roger Horchow tells how he initially invested everything he owned in the Horchow Collection—down to mortgaging his home. And Mary Kay Ash was warned that if her business failed she would lose everything she owned. Similarly, although Mary Hudson had only invested $200 in her first service station, an amount which she had to borrow, a business failure would have wiped her out. Gary Goranson also had to mortgage his home to capitalize his business.

Why were these individuals willing to assume such great personal risk? They had conviction. They *knew* they would succeed. And although some of them had failed in previous ventures, none would ever accept permanent defeat. They were too resilient to be conquered by discouragement. Joe Sugarman shows this when he talks about an early business failure: "That was just one of my incredibly big disappointments. There were other times I felt so sure that I was about to become a millionaire that I started reading the classified ads for mansions and picked up brochures on Cadillacs. Then in the next moment I would totally lose the dream. I would be back to zero and have to start all over again. Thank God I was able to bounce back."

I believe it's important to realize that every one of these twelve entrepreneurs experienced disappointments and setbacks along the way. But they all persevered. Perhaps this ability—to accept failure without admitting defeat—is paramount in achieving long-term success. Roger Horchow explains how he had projected that his business would lose $1 million its first year, break even the second, and turn the corner the third. Instead, as he puts it, "some extraneous activity caused our setback, and it wouldn't be repeated again." Actually, he describes it rather mildly—the company lost another $1 million its second year. However, he was able to discover the cause and turn his business around.

Bill McGowan also met with near-disaster when AT&T challenged certain aspects of the 1971 FCC ruling, and consequently refused permission to interconnect with Bell customer terminals. Bill explains what this meant to his company: "It was somewhat like a long-distance airline . . . the competition owned all the airports and wouldn't allow us to land." By late 1973 MCI had spent $80 million and, because AT&T had refused to interconnect its service, almost went under. Bill explains, "Because we needed working capital to keep the ship afloat, we had to get additional funds from our creditors. And you can imagine how intimidated our customers were—the largest corporation in the world had announced that it didn't want us around. We were facing the worst possible circumstances, because we hadn't finished enough of the system to be viable."

Joe Sugarman may joke about his past failures, but he probably didn't find them a laughing matter at the time. For his first attempt in direct mail he projected that the company needed a return of .2 of one percent to make a profit. The response was only .1 of one percent, and he lost half of his money. However, he didn't become discouraged. Careful analysis showed that two of his ten mailing lists had made money. Zeroing in on these two lists generated a profitable rate of return and launched a successful business career. All these successful entrepreneurs display this kind of stick-to-it-iveness.

Another quality the entrepreneurs share is the willingness to work long, hard hours. Mary Hudson says it best: "In the business world you just can't afford to think about the hours. That's the worst thing you can do. You've got to think about the job, and the work has to be done—regardless of the time it takes!" Early in her career Mary would start at 5:00 in the morning and often work until midnight.

John Galbreath, during the first years of his career, worked twelve to fourteen hours every day of the week and then studied real estate late into the night. At age seventy-seven, W. Clement Stone still puts in a long day, beginning at 8:00 each morning and working until 11:30 at night. He requires a second shift of secretaries to work at his villa following his regular office hours.

Conviction, perseverance, and hard work are certainly necessary to success in any career, but the successful entrepreneur must also be innovative. Each of the twelve people in this book had built a better mousetrap. For his National Revenue Corporation, Richard Schultz developed a more competitive fee structure, one based on a fixed fee instead of the more usual percentage basis. Dale Lang came up with a new way for advertisers to place ads in national magazines in a local area. In the process, through the use of efficient, long-run presses, he lowered the cost from $60 per thousand to $15 per thousand. Gary Goranson devised a superior method of polishing an automobile on the spot, and at a very competitive price. Bill Richards applied many creative techniques to agriculture. For example, he developed a minimum-tillage program, and he was one of the first to use agricultural chemicals. "I was always willing to try new concepts in farming," he explains.

Study the careers of any of these twelve entrepreneurs and you'll discover that they all dared to be different. Mary Hudson came up with many innovative concepts later copied by the giant companies. She built small service-station buildings without bays. She stressed lower prices, and middle-of-the-block locations instead of corners. She believed in wide driveways and good lighting. The result is that Hudson Oil outlets pump 100,000 gallons a month while major oil companies' outlets average 30,000 gallons per month. Bill McGowan believed that MCI Communications could succeed by specializing in telecommunications service for the business community, that good merchandising coupled with products designed to meet the special needs of business would give his company a decisive edge. The most attractive segment of the industry was long-distance service. He claims, "There was no more need to have one company connect all the long-distance services together than there is to have only one airline handle all the commercial airline service in the United States."

John De Lorean is considered one of America's most exciting and creative entrepreneurs. His DMC-12 has gull-wing doors that open upward. Innovative safety features will protect passengers in crashes at speeds up to eighty miles an hour. The car's plastic inner body and stainless-steel skin make it rust-proof. All these features represent new concepts in automotive design, engineering, and construction.

Another quality of these entrepreneurs is their outstanding sales ability. Most credit their success to being supersalespersons. They possess all the necessary ingredients—conviction, enthusiasm, excellent work habits, total commitment, and superior product knowledge. While Joe Sugarman is acknowledged by the advertising industry as one of America's top creators of copy, he considers himself a top salesman rather than an ad man. When asked his secret for successful ads, he says, "The key is knowing how to sell your product. Don't for a moment think it doesn't involve salesmanship."

Supersalesmanship was also required when Dale Lang initially approached national magazines to sell local advertising. "The difficult part," he explains, "was getting publishers to go to bed with each other; getting *Time* and *Newsweek* to participate was like getting Macy's and Gimbels to lie down together. *Time*'s first reaction was, 'It's a great idea, but don't give it to *Newsweek*.' We had to sell both of them on the fact that we weren't going to be part of the competition they had with each other."

Richard Schultz depended on his selling ability when he launched National Revenue. He explains that he overcame the disadvantage of his youth when he recruited a salesman by making him think, "Boy, if this guy could make so much money, I can do it too." Richard would personally take a new salesman into the field to show commissions being earned. "That was the greatest way to recruit," he explains. "I would make $1,000 in commissions in a single day, and the guy would be jumping up and down!"

W. Clement Stone's early career was also dependent on his supersalesmanship. He still gets enthusiastic telling how he once averaged seventy-two policies per day for nine working days. His best day during that period was 122 sales! He used his great talent to convince his sales force that every territory was a good one. "If there was a salesperson or a manager who wasn't producing in an area, I would go out in the field to prove that there was a bonanza in his territory," he declares. "It's really like a game. Naturally, nobody is going to sell everybody. You're going to lose one now and then. But who would want to win every time? It's like playing tennis—you wouldn't want to beat some little kid all the time. You want to have a little competition. When a prospect says no, that's part of the challenge." Evidently Stone was so good that it was rare when he didn't sell a policy to his prospect.

These entrepreneurs follow another pattern—once they found and perfected a formula for success, they would repeat it again and again. In essence, when they had a winner, they stuck with it. W. Clement Stone accumulated one of the larg-

est fortunes in America working on this principle. He stresses, "I don't care what field an individual works in, anyone
who is truly successful develops a formula and scientifically
follows a game plan. I developed a successful sales presentation, and I told every man and woman who came to work for
me, 'If you do exactly as I tell you, you can't fail! Look, you
don't have to believe a thing. I will *prove* it to you . . . I'll
prove that you can do it too.'" He kept emphasizing, "It's
impossible to fail—absolutely impossible! I would even offer
large sums of money to anyone who could show me one failure of any individual in our organization who followed the
system."

Mary Kay Ash also developed an effective sales presentation which was then repeated again and again by the Mary
Kay Cosmetics army of sales representatives. And once Mary
Hudson had developed a successful service-station format,
she continued to follow the formula with new stations. John
Galbreath builds giant high-rise office buildings, and although no two of his skyscrapers are alike, there are definite
principles to which he attributes much of his success. And a
study of Joe Sugarman's ads will show a pattern which he
successfully follows.

Are these entrepreneurs worried that their competition will
copy the successful formulas? Richard Schultz says Kipling's
poem "The 'Mary Gloster'" sums up his attitude: "They
copied all they could follow, but they couldn't copy my
mind,/And I left 'em sweating and stealing, a year and a half
behind." Richard adds, "The company that we are today will
not be able to compete with the company we're going to be a
year from now." The other eleven entrepreneurs were similarly unconcerned about the possibility of competitors dupli-
cating their products or services. All have full confidence in
their continued creative ability.

Many people shy away from beginning an enterprise of
their own because they believe—wrongly—that a great deal
of money is required. It's true that large industrial undertak-

ings demand huge investments, but most of the entrepreneurs in this book started small. Only Bill McGowan, in forming MCI Communications, and John De Lorean, in founding De Lorean Motor Company, required capitalization in the millions of dollars. This is to be expected in capital-intensive industries. Roger Horchow is the only other entrepreneur in the book who had to raise a seven-figure investment. And although Bill Richards invested only $140 per acre in his 300-plus-acre farm in 1954, the cost of purchasing a farm has risen considerably during the past quarter of a century, and large-scale farming today may require a considerable investment.

But most of the businesses in this book were started with a minimum of capital. John Galbreath's only initial investment in real estate was that he put his savings into a car. Mary Hudson invested $200 in her first service station, and W. Clement Stone initially put $100 into his insurance career! Richard Schultz's only investment was $5,000, as was Gary Goranson's—which he borrowed from a local bank. Joe Sugarman began his company with $12,000; Mary Kay Ash made a similar investment. Dale Lang's only investment was the money he had parlayed from the savings he accumulated while working his way through college!

It's apparent that not all business ventures require large capitalization. I believe that many Americans are under the illusion that wealth is necessary in order to enter the arena, but this is obviously not true. While a financial commitment may be required, oftentimes it is another price which must be paid. Hard work, persistence, commitment—this is the *real* investment of every successful entrepreneur.

Finally, let's always remember that the successful entrepreneur is vital to our society. A thriving enterprise benefits the whole community socially, culturally, and economically by providing good salaries as well as opportunities for advancement and education. The entrepreneur makes a central contribution to the health of the free-enterprise system.

About the Author

Robert L. Shook has had a successful sales career since his graduation from Ohio State University in 1959. He is chairman of the board of Shook Enterprises, author of *Ten Greatest Salespersons* and *Winning Images,* and coauthor of *How to Be the Complete Professional Salesman* and *Total Commitment.* He lives in Columbus, Ohio, with his wife and three children.